Shipwrecks, Monsters, and Mysteries of the Great Lakes

ED BUTTS

TUNDRA BOOKS

Published in Canada by Tundra Books,
75 Sherbourne Street, Toronto, Ontario M5A 2P9

Published in the United States by Tundra Books of Northern New York,
P.O. Box 1030, Plattsburgh, New York 12901

Library of Congress Control Number: 2010928786

Library and Archives Canada Cataloguing in Publication

Butts, Edward, 1951–
Shipwrecks, monsters, and disasters
of the Great Lakes / Ed Butts.

ISBN 978-1-77049-206-6

1. Shipwrecks—Great Lakes (North America)—History.
2. Great Lakes (North America)—History. I. Title.

G525.B877 2011   971.3   C2010-903167-9

We acknowledge the financial support of the Government of Canada through the Book Publishing Industry Development Program (BPIDP) and that of the Government of Ontario through the Ontario Media Development Corporation's Ontario Book Initiative. We further acknowledge the support of the Canada Council for the Arts and the Ontario Arts Council for our publishing program.

ONTARIO ARTS COUNCIL
CONSEIL DES ARTS DE L'ONTARIO

Printed and bound in Canada

1 2 3 4 5 6   16 15 14 13 12 11

For Kyle Howell of Cape Breton;
my cousin and a true authority on the Edmund Fitzgerald.

Author's Note

At the time of these events, imperial measurements were used in Canada as they still are in the United States today. To conform to the standards of the times, I have used imperial measurements. The following tables will help if you need a better understanding of distances, temperatures, and weights.

1 inch	=	2.4 centimeters
1 foot	=	30.48 centimeters
1 yard	=	.91 meters
1 mile	=	1.60 kilometers
32 degrees Fahrenheit	=	0.00 degrees Celsius
100 degrees Fahrenheit	=	37.77 degrees Celsius
1 ton	=	1.10 metric tonnes

Contents

Introduction

In 1679, a French ship called the *Griffon,* the first sailing vessel built on the Great Lakes, left Green Bay on Lake Michigan, bound for Niagara with a cargo of furs. The *Griffon* and the five-man crew were never seen again. Though no one knows exactly what happened to the ship, there is no doubt that the *Griffon's* mysterious disappearance was the result of the first shipwreck on the Great Lakes.

Since the loss of the *Griffon,* more than six thousand vessels, large and small, have met tragic ends on the Great Lakes. The bottoms of Lakes Ontario, Erie, Huron, Michigan, and Superior are littered with their wreckage and the bones of the people who sailed on them. Their stories live on in songs and legends that make up the lore of the lakes.

Before railroads and highways were built, the Great Lakes were the principal means of transportation into the heart of North America. Freighters carried timber, grain, ore, livestock, and the products of industry. For hundreds of thousands of immigrants, the Great Lakes were a major leg on their journey west. As commercial traffic grew, small ports became major cities: Toronto, Buffalo, and Chicago, to name a few. People traveling from one Great Lake community to another usually went by boat. Even after the coming of the railroads and highways, shipping remained the cheapest way to transport goods. This was especially true after the St. Lawrence Seaway opened the Great Lakes to ocean-going vessels.

For many years salt-water mariners scoffed at the fresh-water sailors of the Great Lakes. They said the lakes were mere puddles compared to the vast oceans, and were no challenge to real seamen. Sailors who had actually worked on the lakes knew differently.

Even in the best sailing conditions, the skippers of Great Lakes vessels worried about shoals and reefs – uncharted rocks and sandbars that could snare a ship or rip a hull wide open. Unpredictable winds could capsize a vessel in a moment. A ship caught in a storm on the lakes did not have as much room to maneuver as did a ship at sea. Rocky shorelines awaited in every direction. One veteran Atlantic sea captain who had looked down on Great Lakes sailors, said that he had gained a new respect for them after just one rough day on windy Lake Ontario.

Storms that blew in without warning, fog that hung over the water like a thick blanket, and ice that could grind wooden hulls to splinters were the natural perils. But Great Lakes sailors were also endangered by human folly. Ship owners and corporate bosses often placed profit ahead of everything, including the safety of crews and passengers. It wasn't uncommon for captains to sail in dangerous weather against their better judgment because greedy employers did not want to lose money while ships sat in port. This was especially true when the navigation season was nearing its end in stormy November, and captains were pressured into making "one more run" before shipping shut down for the winter. Many vessels lacked safety and emergency equipment because their owners did not want to buy it. Passenger ships were frequently overcrowded when travel companies tried to wring every possible dollar out of a voyage. If a ship did sink, the owners claimed insurance.

Eventually the lakes were completely mapped and charted, and markers and lighthouses warned captains of dangerous rocks and shoals. Technology improved weather-warning systems, and better ship-to-shore communications helped avoid disasters. Seamen's unions fought for improvements in safety, and governments passed laws that prevented some of the worst shipping companies' abuses. But even with all these advances, in many aspects the Great Lakes remain untamed, and any ship venturing out of port into the wilderness of water faces the unexpected.

The Wreck of the Speedy

Foredoomed

Foredoomed is a word seldom used these days. It conjures up images of a by-gone era. However, since the events of this story took place in the early nineteenth century, perhaps it is appropriate to say that the crew of HMS *Speedy*, and all of the people associated with the murder trial of a Native named Ogetonicut were foredoomed. Some accounts say the *Speedy* was unseaworthy. That may have been so. As wooden ships of the time went, she was old, having plied the waters of Lake Ontario for twenty-seven years. It has also been said that had there been a lighthouse on the Presqu'ile Peninsula, the *Speedy* might have reached port safely.

But if the people of the *Speedy* were indeed foredoomed, maybe the friendly beacon of a lighthouse would have made no difference.

The sequence of events that led to the disaster began a year earlier, when Whistling Duck, a member of the Muskrat branch of the Chippewas, was murdered near Lake Scugog, in what was then called Upper Canada. Whistling Duck's brother, Ogetonicut, accused a white man named John Sharp of the crime. Sharp, formerly a soldier with the Queen's Rangers, was the manager of Farewell's trading post at Bull Point on Lake Skugog. Colonial authorities promised Ogetonicut that his brother's slayer would be punished. Had that promise been kept, the *Speedy* tragedy would never have happened. But when a year had passed and John Sharp was still walking around free, Ogetonicut apparently ran out of patience with "white man's justice." Sharp was found beaten and stabbed to death near the trading post, and though there were no eyewitnesses, Ogetonicut was the prime suspect.

White man's justice was not so slow to act when a Native was accused of killing a white man. Shortly after Sharp's murder, a party of Muskrats traveled down to Port Oshawa and then went by canoe to York (Toronto), most likely on a trading mission. They camped at Gibraltar Point on Toronto Island, which at that time was still a peninsula.

Word reached authorities in York that Ogetonicut was in the Native camp, so a party of soldiers was sent to arrest him. There might have been a nasty confrontation, but the Muskrat leader, Chief Wabbekisheco, didn't want

In 1804, the only lighthouse on Lake Ontario was at Mississauga Point at the mouth of the Niagara River. It was torn down for military purposes during the War of 1812. The first permanent lighthouse on the lake was built on Toronto Island's Gibraltar Point in 1808. Colonial governments were often too short of money to construct and maintain lighthouses. Presqu'ile did not get a lighthouse until 1840.

any trouble. He took Ogetonicut by the shoulder and handed him over to the soldiers. The suspect was locked up in the York jail.

Now there was some debate over where the trial should be held. All of the court officials required for the proceeding were there in York, but since the crime had been committed in the district of Newcastle, the trial had to be held there. Newcastle (not to be confused with the present town of Newcastle, Ontario) was a fledgling community on the little Presqu'ile Peninsula, just west of the larger Prince Edward Peninsula. Because roads were poor, the trip to Newcastle would be made by water.

On October 8, 1804, the Provincial Marine schooner HMS *Speedy*, commanded by Lieutenant Thomas Paxton, and with a crew of five, prepared to sail from the port of York, bound for Newcastle, about 100 miles to the east. Accounts disagree as to how many people were on board. Some say twenty, others say thirty-four. Among the passengers were some of Upper Canada's leading men. The trial judge, Justice Thomas Cochrane, originally from Halifax, was only twenty-eight and had already been Chief Justice of Prince Edward Island. Angus McDonell and Robert Isaac Dey Gray were members of the Upper Canada House of Assembly, and Gray was also the colony's Solicitor General. John Fisk was High Constable of York. Also aboard were a fur trader and British Indian Department interpreter, a merchant, Robert Gray's servant, a surveyor who worked for the government, a law student, and the prisoner, Ogetonicut. Two children were placed aboard the schooner by their parents, who could not afford passage for themselves, and so were traveling to Newcastle by land. The parents wanted to spare the children the discomforts of a journey along the rough road.

One man who chose not to go aboard the *Speedy,* but decided instead to travel to Newcastle on horseback, was William Weekes, a lawyer. Originally from Ireland, Weekes had a bizarre episode in his past. He liked to go hunting in the woods alone, and on one occasion was gone for so long that officials suspected foul play. They searched the property of a man named Peter Ernest and found human remains under a pile of logs. Ernest was arrested and charged with the murder of William Weekes. The trial was underway, and things were not going well for Ernest, when the "victim," William Weekes, came strolling into town. Ernest was apparently cleared of any responsibility for the human remains, which might have been very old. By choosing to ride his horse to Newcastle, William Weekes escaped the fate of the people on board the *Speedy.* But destiny had something else in store for him.

Lieutenant Paxton did not want to take so many passengers aboard the *Speedy.* He complained that the schooner was overloaded, and he thought a storm was blowing in. But the Lieutenant Governor of Upper Canada told the captain to get under way or be court martialed.

The *Speedy's* departure was delayed when she ran aground. Once freed, the schooner sailed to Port Oshawa to pick up a pair of brothers named Farewell who had been the murdered Sharp's employers at the trading post. The Farewells did not think the *Speedy* was seaworthy, and refused to go aboard. They chose to accompany the schooner in a canoe. That decision undoubtedly saved their lives.

Because they had started late and conditions on the lake were so poor, by the evening of October 8 the schooner and canoe had gone only as far as Colborne, just to the west of Newcastle. Night was falling and the lake was rough. Nonetheless, both vessels stayed on course for Newcastle. Then the storm Lieutenant Paxton had predicted struck.

The Farewell brothers quickly paddled for shore and found a safe place to wait out the storm. The last they saw of the *Speedy*, she was off Presqu'ile Point, fighting heavy seas. Crosswinds made sailing on Lake Ontario tricky at the best of times. Storm conditions made the lake as deadly as any of the larger Great Lakes, and this storm soon became a blizzard.

Someone on shore claimed to have heard one of the *Speedy's* guns fired as a distress signal. And someone else supposedly lit a bonfire at the tip of Presqu'ile to act as a beacon for the schooner, but to no avail. The *Speedy* and all those on board vanished from the face of the earth. She might have foundered while trying to find the harbor entrance in the dark, or she might have capsized. Schooners on the Great Lakes frequently flipped over when caught by a strong wind from an unexpected quarter. No bodies were ever found. The only clues to the ship's destruction were a mast, a compass box, and a chicken coop.

The sinking of the *Speedy* was a disaster for Upper Canada. The York *Gazette* reported:

> "A more distressing and melancholy event has not occurred to this place for many years; nor does it often happen that such a number of persons of respectability are collected in the same vessel. Not less than nine widows, and we know not how many children, have to lament the loss of their husbands and fathers, who, alas, have, perhaps in the course of a few minutes, met with a watery grave."

It would take the House of Assembly and the Upper Canada legal fraternity some time to recover from the loss of a Solicitor General, a judge, two members of the House of Assembly – all of them lawyers – in one tragic accident. There would be another victim, too. Because of the *Speedy* disaster, the colonial government decided that the harbor of Newcastle was "inconvenient." The town never flourished and most of the people who had settled there moved elsewhere.

William Weekes must have thanked his lucky stars that he had not sailed on the *Speedy*. But two years later, almost to the day, his luck ran out. Weekes got into a quarrel with a man named Dickson in Niagara Falls, and the two gentlemen decided to settle the matter "on the field of honor." Authorities in Upper Canada took a dim view of dueling, so, on the morning of October 10, 1806, Weekes, Dickson and their seconds crossed over to the American side of the river. There they faced each other over pistols and exchanged shots. Weekes missed. Dickson didn't. That night Weekes, who had just been elected to the House of Assembly, died from a gunshot wound. His obituary in the *Oracle,* an early Upper Canadian newspaper, said: "His last moments were marked with that fortitude which was characteristic of his life, convinced of the purity of which, he met death with pleasure."

The last man connected with the Ogetonicut case was dead; foredoomed perhaps, because the white man's justice had failed to act when a white man killed a Native. For the spirit of the murdered Whistling Duck, vengeance was complete.

2

The Scourge and the Hamilton

"A rushing of winds"

On June 18, 1812, after a series of international political crises, the United States declared war on Great Britain. The American government decided that the best way to strike at the British was to attack Britain's North American colonies, Upper and Lower Canada. For an invasion of Upper Canada (Ontario) to succeed, the Americans would have to gain naval control of Lake Ontario and Lake Erie.

The senior American naval officers in charge of operations on Lake Ontario had a problem, however. Commodore Isaac Chauncey and Lieutenant Melancthon T. Woolsey, did not have enough warships to make up a fleet, so they quickly commandeered several merchant vessels and fitted them out as fighting ships. One was the American schooner *Diana,* 112 feet long and weighing 76 tons. Woolsey renamed the vessel the *Hamilton,* after Secretary of the Navy Paul Hamilton, and armed her with nine cannons. Another was the former Canadian schooner *Lord Nelson,* 110 feet long and 45 tons. Just two weeks before the war had started, the American naval brig *Oneida,* commanded by Woolsey, had seized the *Lord Nelson* as a suspected smuggler. Woolsey took the schooner back to the American naval base at Sackets Harbor at the eastern end of Lake Ontario. The *Lord Nelson*'s Canadian owner, James Crooks, protested that his ship had been seized illegally, but to no avail. The schooner was re-named the *Scourge,* mounted with ten cannons, and put into the service of the United States Navy.

Many sailors of that time believed that changing a ship's name brought bad luck. However, it was not superstition that caused problems for the *Scourge* and the *Hamilton,* but their basic design. They were merchant vessels, built to haul cargo. They were not intended to have heavy guns on deck, and their original bulwarks did not provide sufficient protection for gun crews. As part of the refit to transform the vessels into warships, their bulwarks were raised. This, along with the weight of the guns, probably made the schooners top-heavy. Ned Myers, a young sailor assigned to the *Scourge,* wrote:

"This craft was unfit for her duty . . . accommodations were bad enough, and she was so tender that we could do little or nothing with her in a blow. It was often prognosticated that she would prove our coffin."

But until the Americans could build real warships for duty on the Great Lakes, the navy had to make do with converted merchant ships.

In November of 1812 the *Hamilton* participated in naval action off the British stronghold of Kingston. On April 27, 1813, the *Hamilton* and the *Scourge* were part of a flotilla that carried an American army across Lake Ontario to attack York (Toronto), the capital of Upper Canada. The Americans defeated the outnumbered British garrison, captured York, then looted and burned it. The American fleet sailed back across the lake, leaving York a smoking ruin. There would be no more such victories for the *Hamilton* and the *Scourge*.

For much of the summer of 1813, Commodore Chauncey's American fleet and the Royal Navy fleet of British Commodore Sir James Lucas Yeo played a game of cat-and-mouse on Lake Ontario. Each commander tried to keep his ships out of reach of the other fleet's guns, while attempting to maneuver into the most advantageous position for an attack. This continued

When it was captured, the Canadian schooner *Lord Nelson* was carrying a cargo of dry goods, sugar, and liquor. The Americans auctioned the cargo off as contraband. However, in an act of gallantry, Lieutenant Woolsey protected several trunks full of women's clothing that were on the ship. They belonged to a Mrs. McCormick, who lived in Queenston, Upper Canada. Woolsey thought that it would be improper to put a lady's garments up for auction. Mrs. McCormick's clothes were returned to her three years later, after the war ended in 1815. No doubt Mrs. McCormick wad pleased that her wardrobe had not become a prize of war.

until the night of August 7, when both squadrons were in the western end of the lake, just off the mouth of the Niagara River. They anchored for the night, within sight of each other, but out of cannon range. The *Scourge* was commanded by Lieutenant Walter Winter, and the *Hamilton* by Sailing Master Joseph Osgood. Both officers had the honorary rank of captain aboard their ships.

On the evening of the seventh, the weather was very calm and the surface of the lake as smooth as glass. Aboard the *Scourge,* the men sat between the guns to eat their supper because Osgood wanted them to be ready for action at a moment's notice. If the breeze shifted to a direction that favored the American fleet, Commodore Chauncey intended to attack the British that night. George Tumblatt, the chief gunner, wanted to secure the cannons for the night. Captain Osgood said that wasn't necessary because the lake was so calm. He told the men to sleep on deck next to the guns. Then he went below to his cabin. Ned Myers later wrote:

> "One of my messmates, Tom Goldsmith, was captain of the gun
> next to me, and as we sat there finishing our suppers, I says to him,
> 'Tom, bring that rug you pinned at Little York, and that will do for
> both of us to stow ourselves away under.' Tom went down and got
> the rug . . . and it made us a capital bed-quilt. As all hands were
> pretty well tired, we lay down, with our heads on shot-boxes, and
> soon went to sleep."

Some time very early on the morning of August 8, a sudden squall swept onto Lake Ontario. Myers was awakened by rain falling on his face. What had been a quiet evening was about to become a nightmare.

Myers reported later:

> "When I opened my eyes, it was so dark I could not see the length
> of the deck. I arose and spoke to Tom, telling him it was about to

rain, and that I meant to go down and get a nip, out of a little stuff we kept in our mess chest, and I would bring up the bottle if he wanted a taste."

In the darkness Myers groped his way toward the hatch he would have to climb into to get the bottle. Less than a minute had passed since he had been awakened by the rain. He had just put a foot on the ladder to climb down, when, "a flash of lightning almost blinded me. The thunder came at the next instant, and with it a rushing of winds that fairly smothered the clap."

Myers knew at once that the *Scourge* was in trouble, because the sails were set in readiness for a call to battle. He immediately loosened the jibsheet. Then he called on a sailor named Leonard Lewis to help him haul up the lee-topsail-sheet. At the same time, he shouted to the wheelsman to put the helm "hard down."

Myers's brave effort was futile. The sudden blast of wind filled the schooner's sails and forced her over on her beam. Within seconds Myers was up to his chest in water. The *Scourge* had capsized!

The unsecured iron cannons rolled across the deck as the *Scourge* went over on her side. Men who were below deck had no chance to get out. Myers told Lewis to drop the line to the top-sail-sheet and look out for himself. As Myers struggled to get to the bow, the jibsheet, which was flailing in the wind, struck him so hard, he thought it had broken his arm.

"The flashes of lightning were incessant, and nearly blinded me," Myers recalled later. "I heard no hail, no order, no call; but the schooner was filled with the shrieks and cries of men to the leeward, who were lying jammed under the guns, shot-boxes, shot, and other heavy things that had gone down as the vessel fell over."

As the *Scourge* foundered, Myers crawled aft on the upper sides of the bulwarks, "amid a most awful and infernal din of thunder and shrieks, and dazzling flashes of lightning; the wind blowing all the while like a tornado." Myers saw his commander, Joseph Osgood, struggling to escape through a cabin window. "He must have been within six feet of me," Myers reported. But Myers could not help him, and Captain Osgood went down with his ship.

Like most nineteenth-century sailors, Ned Myers could not swim. But he knew that the *Scourge* was going down. In desperation, he jumped into the cold, dark waters of Lake Ontario.

> "I made a spring, therefore, and fell into the water several feet from the place where I had stood. It is my opinion that the schooner sank as I left her. I went down some distance myself, and when I came up to the surface, I began to swim vigorously, for the first time in my life."

By sheer luck Myers found a lifeboat that had not been dragged down by the *Scourge* and climbed into it. "I got in without any difficulty," he recalled, "being all alive and much excited." Myers looked for the *Scourge*. "She had disappeared, and I supposed she was just settling under water." Amidst pouring rain and flashes of lightning, Myers began to search for other survivors.

> "My only chance of seeing was during the flashes, and these left me almost blind . . . I now called out to encourage the men, telling them I was in the boat. I could hear many around me, and occasionally I saw the heads of men struggling in the lake . . . I got an oar in the after rowlock and made out to scull a little in that fashion. I now saw a man quite near the boat, and hauling in the oar, made a spring amidships, catching this poor fellow by the collar. He was very near gone, and I had a great deal of difficulty in getting him in over the gunwale . . . This turned out to be Leonard Lewis, the young man who had helped me to clew up the fore-topsail."

Myers put the oar back in the water and resumed his search. "By my calculation I moved a few yards, and must have got over the spot where the schooner went down. Here in the flashes, I saw many heads, the men swimming in confusion and at random. By this time little was said, the whole scene being one of fearful struggle and frightful silence."

Myers pulled another seven men into the lifeboat, including his messmate Tom Goldsmith. As the survivors rowed through the pitch black night, they were afraid they might be picked up by a British ship and made prisoners of war. Fortunately for them, they encountered the American schooner *Julia,* and were taken aboard.

Crewmen from the *Julia* went out in a lifeboat with a lantern to look for more survivors. They came back with four men, but they weren't from the *Scourge.* The schooner *Hamilton,* too, had capsized! Most of the crew, including Captain Walter Winter, had drowned. Another four of the *Hamilton's* men were picked up by the schooner *Governor Tompkins,* making sixteen the total number of survivors from both vessels. According to many accounts of the disaster, more than one hundred lives were lost. However, records show that the *Hamilton* lost thirty-two men and the *Scourge* lost twenty-one. This was the second-largest loss of life on the Great Lakes during the War of 1812. In the Battle of Lake Erie on September 10, 1813, the Americans had twenty-seven men killed and the British forty.

With two of his ships suddenly gone, Commodore Chauncey could not risk an attack on the British. Oddly, the British did not seem to be aware that the Americans had lost the vessels. Three days later the British captured the American schooners *Growler* and *Julia.* Not until then did British Commodore Yeo mention in his reports that the *Scourge* and the *Hamilton* had sunk.

James Crooks, the original owner of the *Lord Nelson,* maintained for the rest of his life that his ship had been illegally confiscated and that the American navy had committed an act of piracy. He tried, without success, to obtain compensation. His family kept the case alive after his death. In 1930, the American government finally paid over $23,000 to Crooks' descendants.

The story of the two ships did not end there. In 1973, a Canadian government research vessel using sonar discovered the wrecks of the *Scourge* and *Hamilton*. Unmanned dives revealed the ships sitting on the lakebed at a depth of 300 feet, and not far apart. The water is dark and cold, so the ships are well preserved. Photographs showed skeletal remains, cannons, cutlasses, axes, spars, and a hat. The ships' interiors will certainly contain many items that will provide valuable information about life in the nineteenth century. The wrecks are in Canadian waters, and are protected by the Department of Culture and Recreation through the *Hamilton − Scourge* project of the city of Hamilton, Ontario.

3

The Lady Elgin

Death in the Darkness

Captain Jack Wilson was growing impatient. It was nearing 11 p.m. on Friday, September 7, 1860, and his ship, the *Lady Elgin,* was scheduled to depart Chicago's harbor at 11 for the short run to Milwaukee. Then she'd be bound up Lake Michigan to Mackinac, the Soo, and Lake Superior. But there were still a lot of visitors on board, partying with the passengers.

The *Lady Elgin* was an American side-wheel steamer, named after the wife of the Governor General of Canada as a gesture of good will. She was one of the most popular excursion ships on the lakes. The owners of the *Lady Elgin* proudly called her "The Queen of the Lakes." Not quite ten years old, the 252-foot-long steamer was luxuriously fitted out with comfortable cabins, saloons, and a dance hall. She could accommodate up to three hundred passengers, along with her crew of forty-five. Like every other passenger ship on the Great Lakes, the *Lady Elgin* also hauled cargo and livestock.

Captain Wilson blew the ship's whistle repeatedly. This was a warning to non-passengers that the ship was about to get underway. The revelers either did not hear the whistle above the din of laughter and music, or they chose to ignore it. This would cost many of them their lives.

Among those whooping it up on the *Lady Elgin* that night were three hundred members of a military organization called the Union Guards of Milwaukee. They had been in Chicago for parades and rallies, and were now returning home. But a lot of their Chicago friends had gone aboard to carry on the celebrations that had begun ashore. It seemed they had no

The invention of the steam engine meant that ships no longer had to depend on wind. Engines turned paddlewheels to propel ships through the water. Two types of paddle wheelers were developed. Stern-wheelers were usually used on rivers, such as the Mississippi. On the Great Lakes, side-wheelers were found to be more efficient. Some ships used a combination of steam and wind power to conserve fuel.

intention of leaving as long as the ship's bartender, a Mr. Lacy, kept the beer and whiskey flowing.

Besides the Union Guards, there were about fifty passengers who were making an excursion up the Lakes. Eliza Curtain, twenty-one, hadn't wanted to go on the trip at all, but her mother had insisted. Another passenger, twenty-three-year-old Cyrus H. Walrath, had originally booked passage on another ship. Then for some reason he had transferred to the *Lady Elgin*. A British Member of Parliament, Herbert Ingram, was enjoying a holiday with his sixteen-year-old son. Colonel Francis A. Lumsden, a publisher from New Orleans, was traveling with his wife and two children. John Jervis was aboard with his wife and her sister, Agnes Keogh.

The scheduled time of departure passed. Captain Wilson, a veteran skipper with twenty-four years of sailing the Lakes behind him, knew there were too many people on the ship. But he couldn't wait any longer. Any visitors who hadn't already disembarked would just have to get off at Milwaukee. At 11:30 the *Lady Elgin* steamed out of Chicago and into the darkness of Lake Michigan.

Also on the lake, but downward bound for Chicago with a cargo of timber, was the 128-foot American schooner *Augusta*. Her skipper, Captain Darius Nelson, "Nelse," Malott, from Essex County, Ontario, was only twenty-seven years old. But he was a capable seaman who'd already had his share of adventure. Nelse Malott had sailed around the world. He had been

Great Lakes sailors in the nineteenth century, like mariners all around the world, were often very transient, moving from one ship to another as they traveled the length and breadth of the lakes. Some did not even use their real names, but might only be known as "Smitty" or "Red" or "Slim." The crews of many vessels would be made up of both Canadians and Americans. Ship owners and captains generally didn't care where a man came from, as long as he did his job well.

shipwrecked twice. On one of those occasions, he had narrowly escaped being killed and eaten by desperate, starving shipmates.

Captain Malott was new to the *Augusta*. He had not had an opportunity to learn his ship's strengths and weaknesses. One of the schooner's problems was that she did not steer very well when laden with cargo, as she was on this trip. The first and second mates, John Vorce and George Budge, had been on the *Augusta* for a long time. They knew of the problem with the helm. But for some reason, they did not tell their new skipper.

In the early hours of Saturday, September 8, a squall swept across Lake Michigan. Strong winds transformed the surface into a mass of heaving waves. Driving rain reduced visibility to almost zero. Lightning flashes gave momentary glimpses of a lake that had suddenly become a sailor's nightmare.

On the *Lady Elgin,* the pitching and rolling of the ship left some of the passengers prone with seasickness. Still, others continued to dance the night away, in spite of the unsteady deck. Ship's policeman Thomas Cummings decided that things had quieted down enough for him to take a break from his duties. He relaxed in a chair in a small cabin just forward of the side-wheel on the port side, and dozed off.

On the *Augusta*, Second Mate Budge was on duty, the captain and first mate having retired for the night. Ten minutes before the storm hit, he saw the red and green running lights of the *Lady Elgin* off in the distance. Although it was his duty to inform the captain that another ship was nearby, Budge did not tell the captain or the first mate. Nor did he order a change of course, even though the ship was directly in the *Augusta's* path. The law at that time required steamers to give the right-of-way to sailing vessels.

In accordance with the law, the *Augusta* had a single white light shining from her bow. But with a heavy sea running and sheets of rain pouring down, it would have been difficult for anyone on the *Lady Elgin* to see the *Augusta's* light. By the time someone on the steamer did spot the light, a collision was unavoidable.

When the squall hit, Captain Malott and First Mate Vorce hurried out on deck to haul in sails. No sooner had the skipper emerged from his cabin, than a powerful gust of wind forced the schooner over on her port side, almost capsizing her. Then a sailor cried out that there was a light off the lee bow. Malott and Vorce looked, and to their horror saw the lights of the big paddle wheeler directly in front of the *Augusta*.

"Hard up, hard up! For God's sake, hard up!" the captain cried to his wheelsman.

It was too late! The *Augusta* was already too close to the *Lady Elgin*. Not responding to the helm, the schooner was driven like an arrow straight at the steamer. The *Augusta's* long jib boom pierced the wooden hull of the *Lady Elgin* just forward of the port side-wheel.

In his cabin, Thomas Cummings was jarred awake when the jib boom of the *Augusta* smashed through the wall and penetrated the bulkhead on the other side of the room. He'd come within inches of being impaled. The pounding seas caused the boom to stab deeper into the *Lady Elgin,* wreaking more damage. Then, when a surge of water pulled the schooner free, the boom ripped a huge hole in the side of the paddle wheeler. Water poured in. The *Lady Elgin* was doomed.

For brief seconds the two vessels were side-by-side. The men on the *Augusta* were certain that their ship had been badly damaged and was in danger of sinking. They called out to the crew of the *Lady Elgin* to throw them a line. There was no response. Then the wind drove the schooner away from the steamer. To the crew of the *Augusta*, it appeared that the *Lady Elgin* was simply continuing on her way.

Aboard the *Augusta,* Captain Malott was furious that the *Lady Elgin* did not stay to assist him. Nobody on the schooner was aware of how badly the steamer had been damaged. They thought that the *Lady Elgin* had been pierced high up, well above the waterline. They thought themselves to be in far greater danger than the big paddle wheeler.

An inspection of the *Augusta's* bow revealed that the damage was not as serious as the crew had first feared. Captain Malott took his vessel on to

Chicago, where he reported the collision. Even if he had been aware that the *Lady Elgin* was, in fact, sinking, it was not likely that his sailing vessel could have gone to the steamer's aid in the storm.

The accident had happened about 10 miles off Winnetka, Illinois. *Lady Elgin*'s First Mate George Davis immediately changed course for shore while Captain Wilson went below to inspect the damage. The skipper saw at once that the situation was bad—extremely bad!

In an effort to lighten the ship, Wilson ordered his crew to throw cargo overboard. This included thirty head of cattle. The men tried to carry out the order, but managed to jettison only one cow. The terrified animals struggled and went sliding across the deck as the *Lady Elgin* listed to the port side.

In desperation Captain Wilson sent men over the side in a lifeboat to try to patch up the hole with sails or mattresses. It was useless! The *Lady Elgin* was going down too quickly. Within minutes the engine room was flooded, and the Queen of the Lakes was dead in the water.

The steamer had only three lifeboats and four yawls (small sailboats); not nearly enough for all of the people on board. The crew hastily began passing out life-preserver floats. These were wooden planks, 5 feet long and a foot wide with ropes at both ends. A float could only support one person.

As his ship sank, Captain Wilson encouraged male passengers to help the crew get women and children off. He passed out floats and told people to remain calm. He said that they were not far from shore. "Hold onto anything that floats," he told them, "and you will make it."

But even though there was no general panic among the passengers of the *Lady Elgin,* there were problems with the evacuation. Many women, including John Jervis's wife and sister-in-law, did not want to leave their cabins. Jervis had to carry his wife and her sister up to the main deck. A man named Timothy O'Brion helped to launch one of the lifeboats. When he went back to get his wife and daughter, the press of passengers rushing for the lifeboats was so great that he could not push his way through. He never saw his wife and child again.

The *Lady Elgin* sank so swiftly that the pressure of air and water from below literally blew the hurricane deck free from the main structure of the ship. While the hull was swallowed up by Lake Michigan, the deck remained afloat. Scores of frightened, screaming people clung to it. Then the pounding of the waves tore that life raft to pieces.

"Hang on tight!" Captain Wilson cried, as people were plunged into the cold, black water. It was utter chaos, with people and cattle thrashing in the dark as lightning flashed and thunder boomed. John Jervis hugged a piece of floating debris while his wife held fast to him. Agnes Keogh held firmly to her sister. Then a wave tore her loose, and she was gone. In the pitch black of the night, men, women, and children cried out for help. They could barely be heard above the shriek of the storm. The squall was now a full-fledged gale.

Those who had survived the sinking of the *Lady Elgin* clung to wreckage that was being carried by wind and wave toward shore. The ones who had made it to lifeboats had no oars. Some of the boats were quickly swamped. Lake Michigan would reap a dreadful toll that September night.

Captain Wilson was on a piece of the hurricane deck with about forty other people. By the time they neared the shore, only eight were left. Then, when the little group was in the breakers and tantalizingly close to land, one woman slipped off, and Captain Wilson dove after her. Both drowned.

Now those who were still alive were in the clutches of a boiling surf. Many were dragged down by the powerful undertow. Others were battered by pieces of debris. John Jervis made it to dry land. His wife did not. A man named James Rodee floated ashore on a drum from the ship's band. Many others were not so fortunate.

The British politician Herbert Ingram was dead, along with his son. So was Cyrus H. Walrath, who had transferred to the *Lady Elgin* from another ship. Eliza Curtain, the young woman who had been reluctant to go on a boating excursion, washed up on the beach, dead. So did Colonel Francis A. Lumsden. His wife and children were also lost.

First Mate Davis reached shore in a lifeboat. He and the people with him quickly fanned out in search of farmhouses and help. Before dawn, word of the calamity reached Winnetka and nearby communities. Rescuers hurried to the lakeshore with ropes, clothing, and blankets. These good Samaritans found to their disgust that scavengers had been there ahead of them.

Many of the bodies on the beach had been plundered of money and jewelry. One was that of bartender Lacy, who had been wearing a money belt stuffed with cash and gold coins. There was evidence that plunderers had ignored the helpless people in the water, while going after kegs of liquor and other salvage.

No one knew for certain just how many men, women, and children died in the wreck of the *Lady Elgin*. The death toll was estimated at between two hundred and seventy-nine and three hundred and fifty. The presence on the ship of so many unregistered guests made an exact count impossible. Also, because so many of those who made it ashore immediately left the vicinity, there could be no exact count of survivors. Authorities estimated the number to be between one hundred and one hundred and fifty.

Augusta's captain, Nelse Malott, was arrested and charged with responsibility for the disaster. In terms of loss of life, the wreck of the *Lady Elgin* was the worst catastrophe ever to occur on the Great Lakes up to that time. There was anger in port communities all around the Lakes, but especially in Milwaukee, which had been home to so many of the dead and missing.

Ugly stories began to circulate. People said that the *Augusta* had been sailing with no lights at all. They muttered that Malott had refused to heave to, and go to the aid of the stricken steamer. Death threats were made against the young skipper.

However, an official inquest cleared Captain Malott of blame. Second Mate Budge was reprimanded for not immediately informing his captain of the *Lady Elgin's* lights. The inquest jury decided that the main cause of the accident lay with the navigation laws, which did not require a ship like the *Augusta* to display adequate lighting at night.

After the *Lady Elgin* tragedy, the *Augusta* was sold. The new owners changed her name to *Colonel Cook*, but had a difficult time hiring crews. Sailors considered her a bad luck ship. They believed she was haunted by the ghosts of the people who died in the *Lady Elgin* disaster. In 1894 the *Colonel Cook* was wrecked on a Lake Erie shoal.

Although Captain Malott had been exonerated, in the end he shared the same unhappy fate as Captain Wilson. On September 8, 1864 – exactly three years after the *Lady Elgin* went down – Nelse Malott, captain of the bark *Mojave,* sailed out of a Lake Michigan port. The ship, captain and crew were never seen again.

4

The Waubuno Mystery
A Georgian Bay Disaster

Often called "the sixth Great Lake," Georgian Bay is considered an extension of Lake Huron, but in reality, it is almost as large in surface area as Lake Ontario. Looking at a map of Lake Huron, you might think that the Bruce Peninsula and Manitoulin Island would shelter Georgian Bay from the worst effects of storms on the open lake. To some degree they do. But Georgian Bay is so large, it can be whipped into a fury all its own. Danger to navigation lies not only with the elements, but also with the geographical nature of the bay. Georgian Bay is a maze of islands, shoals, and reefs that lie in ambush for unwary vessels.

This was especially true in the nineteenth century, when Great Lakes ships were made of wood, and many of the bay's hidden dangers were not yet charted. However, water was still the quickest and cheapest means of transportation for people and cargo. The roads connecting communities like Collingwood, Midland, and Parry Sound were of very poor quality. Rather than take a time-consuming, uncomfortable, and costly trip by land, most people preferred to go by ship. The *Waubuno*, a very familiar vessel to those Georgian Bay travelers, is central to one of the greatest unsolved mysteries of Georgian Bay.

The *Waubuno* was a side-wheel steamer, built in Thorold, Ontario, in 1865. Her name was somewhat ominous. According to Algonquin lore, a *waubuno* was the Native version of a warlock – a practitioner of black magic. Only 135 feet long and 19 feet in the beam, the 465-ton *Waubuno* was small. For several years she braved the open waters of Lake Huron and Lake Superior. But wooden Great Lakes ships aged quickly. By 1879 the *Waubuno* was making the relatively easy run on Georgian Bay between Collingwood and Parry Sound. She was still a seaworthy vessel after fourteen years of hard service, but her owners considered her better suited to the waters of Georgian Bay than the heavy seas of the open lakes.

At noon on November 21, 1879, the *Waubuno* was in port at Collingwood. It was late in the season, when bad weather often disrupted sailing schedules. The *Waubuno* was loaded with freight, including several head of horses and cattle. A large number of passengers had boarded the steamer for the trip to Parry Sound. But for the time being the *Waubuno* wasn't going anywhere.

A shrieking gale had been tearing into Georgian Bay since the night before. George Burkett, the thirty-three-year-old captain of the *Waubuno* could not cast off until the weather cleared. Some passengers complained about the delay. Others thought Captain Burkett was showing good sense. Better to wait out the storm, they said, than to risk the furious waters of the bay.

Among the passengers was a young newlywed couple, Dr. W.D. Doupe and his wife. They were on their way to tiny McKellar Village, well off in the bush beyond Parry Sound, where Dr. Doupe, fresh out of medical school, intended to establish his practice. According to a story that would circulate later, Mrs. Doupe was upset because of a terrible nightmare she had suffered the previous evening. As she and her husband slept in their cabin while the *Waubuno* was tied to the Collingwood dock, she had dreamed that the *Waubuno* was shipwrecked, and she, her husband, and everyone else on board were drowned!

The dream had seemed so real, that in the morning Mrs. Doupe begged her husband to take them off the *Waubuno* and wait for another ship. The doctor dismissed his wife's fears as ridiculous. He wasn't about to change their travel planes just because of a dream. Their luggage and furniture, as well as the equipment for his medical office, had already been loaded aboard the *Waubuno*.

Captain Burkett allegedly heard the couple arguing in the companionway. He assured Mrs. Doupe that they would not sail until it was safe to do so. Mrs. Doupe calmed down, and agreed to say no more about the matter. She went back to their cabin to nervously wait out the storm. But the story of Mrs. Doupe's frightening dream quickly spread through the ship.

As the afternoon dragged into the evening and the storm showed no signs of abating, many of the passengers left the *Waubuno* for accommodations in town. They thought it unlikely that the *Waubuno* would sail before morning. Rather than spend the night aboard a ship that was being buffeted by wind and waves, they preferred to sleep in the comfort of the Globe Hotel or the homes of friends or relatives. No doubt a few who had been unnerved by the story of Mrs. Doupe's dream found this a good excuse to get off the *Waubuno*. However, Dr. and Mrs. Doupe slept in their cabin.

Captain Burkett had something more substantial than Mrs. Doupe's bad dream to worry about. Another steamer, the *Magnettawan,* had recently begun competing with the *Waubuno* for passenger and cargo business and she was newer and faster than the *Waubuno.* At that moment the *Magnettawan* was also at the Collingwood dock, scheduled to sail at ten o'clock in the morning. The *Waubuno*'s owners had been complaining to Captain Burkett that the *Magnettawan* had been beating the *Waubuno* to ports and scooping up the awaiting passengers and cargoes. Captain Burkett might have been thinking that if he didn't get a head start on the *Magnettawan* for this run, it would happen again.

By three o'clock on the morning of November 22ⁿᵈ, the storm had died down considerably. Captain Burkett roused his crew and told them to prepare to get underway. He was told that his wheelsman had left the ship and wasn't coming back, stating that he had decided to "call it a season." Perhaps the man had heard of Mrs. Doupe's dream. Captain Burkett decided it didn't matter. He knew how to handle a ship's wheel.

By four o'clock the *Waubuno* was ready to depart. A few of the passengers who had gone to the hotel had been informed that the *Waubuno* was getting up steam, and they had hurried to the dock to get aboard. The captain decided not to wait for the others. The *Waubuno*'s lines were cast off, and the steamer slid out of port and into the darkness of Georgian Bay. A handful of passengers who had learned too late that the *Waubuno* was leaving rushed down to the dock only to find their ship had gone. They were angry, but they didn't yet know that they were the lucky ones.

Twenty-four people were aboard the *Waubuno* as she steamed north from Collingwood toward Christian Island: fourteen crewmen including Captain Burkett, and ten passengers including Dr. and Mrs. Doupe. Christian Island lay about one-third of the way to Parry Sound. John Hoar, the lighthouse keeper there, saw the *Waubuno*'s lights as she passed. He reported in his log, "A stiff wind from the nor'west but ship seemed to be riding well with full cargo." After that, no known person ever saw the *Waubuno* again.

Once he had passed Christian Island, Captain Burkett evidently decided not to stay on the usual route to Parry Sound. Taking that course would have meant crossing twenty-eight miles of open water between Hope Island and Lone Rock. The *Waubuno* would have been exposed to the full force of that stiff nor'wester John Hoar noted in his log. Instead, the captain chose to steer for Moose Point and take the South Channel. This route was protected from the worst of the strong winds. But it was also a gauntlet of reefs and shoals. Even if a skipper knew those waters well, as Captain Burkett undoubtedly did, he still needed good visibility to navigate through them safely.

Visibility must have been reasonably good when the *Waubuno* entered the South Channel. But then snow began to fall heavily, and the strong winds turned the snowfall into a blizzard. Out on the water, visibility would have been reduced to almost zero. The *Waubuno* would have been sailing blind along a course riddled with traps!

At about noon that day, some lumbermen working on Moose Point heard the blasts of a ship's whistle. They thought the sounds came from a ship signaling someone on an island, which was a common practice in those days. What they most likely heard were distress signals from the *Waubuno,* the only ship that could have been in the vicinity at that time. Even if the lumbermen had recognized the signals as a call for assistance, they would not have been able to help the people on the *Waubuno.*

Back in Collingwood, the *Magnettawan* left on schedule at ten o'clock in the morning. She hadn't gone very far before Captain John O'Donnell decided that Georgian Bay was still too rough for a safe crossing. His ship was being tossed on heavy seas and his passengers were seasick. Captain O'Donnell took his ship to shelter in the lee of Christian Island to await better weather. Forty hours passed before the *Magnettewan* could finally complete the voyage to Parry Sound. The storm that Captain O'Donnell had wisely waited out was one of the worst ever to fall upon Georgian Bay.

When the *Magnettawan* steamed into Parry Sound at noon on November 24th, Captain O'Donnell expected to see the *Waubuno* at the dock. He soon learned that she had not arrived at all. A tugboat and many smaller craft searched the South Channel. The would-be rescuers hoped that the *Waubuno* had been driven ashore, and that her people would be safe in some isolated cove or inlet. But all the searchers found was evidence of a shipwreck.

Thousands of apples, part of the *Waubuno*'s cargo, had washed ashore. So had crates of calico and clothing bound for general stores in communities around the bay. Amazingly, the searchers recovered every one of the *Waubuno*'s life jackets. Whatever disaster had struck the ship had happened so fast that nobody had even had a chance to put them on. No survivors were found – and not a single body.

Four months later, the *Waubuno*'s hull was discovered floating upside down in an isolated, quiet little bay near Moose Point. The hull was an empty shell. All of the cabins and the ship's machinery were gone. Just to the west of where the hull was found lay a deadly shoal, known today as the Haystacks. In 1879, that shoal had not yet been charted, so Captain Burkett would not have known about it. In 1962, SCUBA divers found one of the *Waubuno*'s anchors near the Haystacks.

No one will ever know for sure what happened to the *Waubuno*, but based on the evidence, Great Lakes historians have been able to piece together a very possible scenario. They believe Captain Burkett was a good distance into the

Although the hull and other parts of the *Waubuno* were eventually found, the superstructure, which most likely contained the bodies, never was. In the 1960s a diver named John Morris thought he saw what might have been part of the *Waubuno*'s superstructure sticking up from a silty bottom. Unfortunately, when Morris returned to the surface, his boat was gone. He drifted for hours before a passing boater picked him up. He could never find the spot again, and believed that the current that had exposed the wreck had quite likely covered it back up.

South Channel when the blizzard struck. Unable to see what was in front of him, he turned back. In the blinding snowstorm the captain ran the *Waubuno* onto the Haystacks. Out of desperation he dropped his anchors and sounded the distress signal. That was the sound the lumbermen had heard. The *Waubuno* capsized within moments of hitting the shoal. The cabins were torn away from the main deck, and the ship's engines and other machinery plunged to the bottom of the bay. The passengers, trapped in their cabins, were also carried down.

That, at least, is the most accepted theory. But it does not satisfactorily explain why no bodies were ever found. Passengers like Dr. and Mrs. Doupe might have been shut up in their cabins, but Captain Burkett and his crew were not. Of course, there had been other wrecks on the Great Lakes in which no bodies had been found, but in Georgian Bay it was unusual. Ordinarily, at least some of the dead would wash up on the mainland shore or on one or more of the many islands.

The story of Mrs. Doupe's prophetic dream certainly adds drama to the story of the *Waubuno,* but not everybody accepts it as true. The *Waubuno*'s anchor can be seen today in Parry Sound's town square. The water in which the steamer is believed to have foundered is now called Waubuno Channel, and a shoal near the place where the ship might have gone down has been named Burkett's Rock.

5

The Bannockburn Mystery

Ghost Ship

For as long as sailors have navigated the seas there have been stories of ghost ships; phantoms of lost vessels that mysteriously appear and then vanish into the mist. Perhaps the most notorious of these apparitions was the *Flying Dutchman,* a ghostly sailing ship supposedly sighted on the high seas many times over hundreds of years. According to the legend, any sailor unlucky enough to see the *Flying Dutchman* will die before he can set foot on dry land again. The Great Lakes, too, have tales of ghost ships. The most famous of these stories is that of the *Bannockburn,* a ship now known in lore as the *Flying Dutchman* of Lake Superior.

The *Bannockburn* was a sturdy steel freighter, built in Scotland in 1893. She was what sailors then called a "canaller;" specially constructed to haul large cargoes, but still fit the locks of the Welland Canal and the canals that bypassed the rapids of the St. Lawrence River before the St. Lawrence Seaway was constructed. The *Bannockburn* was 245 feet long, 40 feet in the beam, and weighed 1,620 tons. In 1902, the world's largest maritime insurance company, Lloyd's of London, rated the *Bannockburn* an A-1 vessel.

Owned by the Montreal Transportation Company of Kingston, Ontario, the *Bannockburn* plied the Great Lakes for nine years, hauling cargoes of grain. She was one of those vessels that could be relied upon to make a successful voyage even in stormy November, when the shipping season was drawing to a close. This tough freighter could take anything that even mighty Lake Superior could throw at her. Or could she?

At 9 a.m. on November 21st, 1902, the *Bannockburn* sailed from Port Arthur, Ontario, on Lake Superior. In the hold were 85,000 bushels of wheat. The *Bannockburn* was bound for Midland, on Georgian Bay. It was late in the season. This would probably be her last run of the year.

The *Bannockburn*'s captain was George R. Wood, from Port Dalhousie (now part of St. Catharines), Ontario. At age thirty-seven, Captain Wood was the oldest man aboard the ship. Many ship owners preferred to hire very young men and even boys, because they could get away with paying them less than they would have to pay older, more experienced sailors.

Most of the *Bannockburn's* crew of twenty-one were between the ages of seventeen and twenty. Wheelsman Arthur Callaghan was only sixteen. As they left Port Arthur that morning, the captain and the young men of his crew had no idea that their destiny was to become part of an intriguing mystery.

In 1970, the Ontario towns of Port Arthur and Fort William were merged to form the modern city of Thunder Bay. Thunder Bay is the Canadian Lakehead on Lake Superior. The American Lakehead on Superior is the city of Duluth, Minnesota.

Late that afternoon at a location about fifty miles southeast of Passage Island and to the northeast of the tip of Michigan's Keweenaw Peninsula, the *Bannockburn* was sighted by Captain James McMaugh of the steamer *Algonquin*. The *Algonquin* was heading for Port Arthur to pick up a cargo of grain, and Captain McMaugh saw the *Bannockburn* at about the place she should have been if Captain Wood had been keeping a steady course and speed.

In his log Captain McMaugh recorded that at the time he saw the *Bannockburn*, visibility on the lake was hazy. He was looking out the window of the pilothouse with his binoculars, and recognized the *Bannockburn's* distinctive three-masted profile. Captain McMaugh was a veteran Great Lakes mariner, and he was familiar with the outlines of most of the big ships.

The two ships passed with a wide distance between them. Captain McMaugh saw that the *Bannockburn* was bucking a strong headwind and ploughing through the choppy waters that were typical of the lake in late November. The *Algonquin* was making good time through those same rough waters, and it did not appear to Captain McMaugh that the *Bannockburn* was in any kind of trouble. Then he turned his head to tell the first mate to take a look at the *Bannockburn*. Both men looked. The ship that had been there just seconds earlier had disappeared! Captain McMaugh was startled and commented, "I must say, that vessel certainly has gotten out of sight remarkably quickly."

The captain and mate decided that the *Bannockburn* had become enveloped in mist, and then put her out of mind. The weather was starting to deteriorate, and they wanted to make Port Arthur before a storm blew in. By the time the *Algonquin* docked in Port Arthur that night, a full-blown gale was raging on Lake Superior. It was not the worst storm ever to hit the lake, but it was bad enough for veteran sailors to call it a "banger." Lake Superior bangers usually sent ships scurrying for the safety of the nearest port.

The next day the *Bannockburn* was reported overdue at Sault Ste. Marie, where she would have had to pass through the locks for the voyage down to Lake Huron. Captain McMaugh was the only man aboard the *Algonquin* who had seen the *Bannockburn* the previous day. Some people believed he only *thought* he had seen the missing ship, but the captain said he was absolutely sure of what he had seen. If so, he may well have been the last person ever to look upon the *Bannockburn* – unless it was a night watchman on the passenger steamer *Huronic*. He had been on duty the stormy night of November 21/22, and saw the lights of a ship he believed was the *Bannockburn*.

Before the day was out there were many strange and false reports in circulation concerning the missing ship. One said the *Bannockburn* had taken shelter in the lee of Slate Island. Another claimed the *Bannockburn* had run aground on the mainland near Michipicoten Island. Yet another said the *Bannockburn* had run aground on Michipicoten Island itself, but that the crew was safe. That report was said to have come from the captain of the steamship *Germanic*. But when contacted about it, the *Germanic's* skipper said he had not made any such report. He had not seen the *Bannockburn* aground at Michipicoten Island or anywhere else. If he had seen the ship aground, he said, he would have investigated it.

Days passed and there was no sign anywhere of the *Bannockburn* or her crew. People in Michipicoten said they had not seen the vessel. If the *Bannockburn* had in fact gone aground somewhere on the mainland shore, the men would have walked to the nearest community. Several tugboats made a thorough search of the waters around Michipicoten Island and Caribou

Island, but found nothing. Then the freighter *Frank Rockefeller* arrived at Sault Ste. Marie with news of some wreckage in the water just off Stannard Rock, one of the most deadly shoals in Lake Superior (now marked by a lighthouse). However, there was nothing in the wreckage to indicate that it had come from the *Bannockburn*. In fact, the only relics known to be from the *Bannockburn* that ever turned up were a lifejacket and an oar that were found on the Michigan shore several months after the ship vanished. Not a single body was ever recovered.

What happened to the *Bannockburn?* Whatever calamity befell the ship, it sank her so quickly that the crew had no time to launch a lifeboat or even put on lifejackets. The lifejackets would have kept the men afloat, so that even if they died from exposure in the cold water, bodies would have washed ashore somewhere. Most likely the men were all carried to the bottom with their ship.

There have been several theories as to the cause of the shipwreck. Captain McMaugh believed that moments after he sighted the *Bannockburn*, an explosion in the boiler room tore the bottom out of the ship, causing her to sink instantly. That, he said, would explain why she disappeared from view so suddenly.

But the *Bannockburn* was only nine years old, and her equipment was in good condition. Lloyd's of London had given the ship its highest rating. On the other hand, profit-hungry ship owners of the time were notorious for skimping on the maintenance of their vessels to keep costs down. Maybe the *Bannockburn* had problems of which the insurance company was unaware. But if Captain McMaugh's theory was correct, what ship's lights did the watchman on the *Huronic* see later that night? There didn't appear to have been any other large vessels in the vicinity.

The crew of the steamer *Frank Rockefeller* had spotted wreckage floating near Stannard Rock. The *Bannockburn's* course would not have taken her anywhere near that fearsome ship-killer, but currents could have carried the debris there from another notorious ship-trap – Caribou Island. This tiny islet surrounded by deadly reefs had a lighthouse to warn ships away from the treacherous waters. But for reasons never explained, the Canadian government had decided to close down the Caribou Island lighthouse early that year, even though shipping was still active on Lake Superior. In the absence of a guiding light, the *Bannockburn* could have smashed into the Caribou Island reefs during the storm.

A few weeks after the *Bannockburn* was lost, the Canadian lock at Sault Ste. Marie was drained for the winter. A steel plate from a ship's hull was found on the bottom of the canal. Could it have fallen off the *Bannockburn* while she passed through on the way to Port Arthur? If so, just how vulnerable would the loss of that plate have made the ship's hull?

Whether or not that plate came from the *Bannockburn,* it's possible that the freighter had a serious structural problem. Just before sailing from Port Arthur, the *Bannockburn* ran aground. After she pulled free, there was a quick inspection for damage. However, by that time the cargo hold was full of grain, and the ship was riding low in the water. The inspection, therefore, could not have been thorough. Perhaps there was damage that under normal circumstances would not have rendered the ship unseaworthy, but that left her too weak to withstand the storm. Unless the remains of the *Bannockburn* should one day be found on the deep, dark bottom of Lake Superior, the mystery may never be solved.

The *Bannockburn*'s story did not end with her sudden disappearance. Since 1903, there have been numerous reports of people seeing a "ghost

Captain Wood's hometown was Port Dalhousie on Lake Ontario. It is now part of the city of St. Catharines. In St. John's Anglican Church there, a tablet dedicated to his memory can still be seen. It reads: IN MEMORIAM, CAPT. GEORGE RICHARD WOOD, BORN MAR. 9, 1865. DIED NOV. 22, 1902. ERECTED BY HIS BROTHER, JOHN W. WOOD.

ship" they believe to be the *Bannockburn*. Sailors on ships and people on shore have claimed they have seen the phantom *Bannockburn* gliding through the mist-shrouded, black waters of Lake Superior, doomed to a never-ending search for a safe port. Some people have even said they could see the haggard faces of Captain Wood and some of his sailors peering out through the windows of the pilothouse, as though searching in vain for the friendly beacon of a lighthouse.

The Wreck of the Monarch

Ordeal on Isle Royale

In the late nineteenth century, as shipping traffic increased on Lake Superior, a three-mile wide strait between the eastern tip of the American Isle Royale and tiny Passage Island became an important short-cut for Canadian ships sailing to and from the ports of Fort William and Port Arthur (now Thunder Bay). This short-cut took the Canadian ships through American waters, but it trimmed fifty miles off the route between the Canadian Lakehead and Sault Ste. Marie. However, it was a dangerous route because of a shoal called Canoe Rock and other deadly reefs. To help guide ships through the hazardous strait, the American government built a lighthouse on Passage Island.

Although the Passage Island lighthouse was a major aid to shipping in the northwestern part of Lake Superior, at times it was but a feeble defense against the fury of Superior and the lurking rocks. In 1906, Isle Royale became the scene of one of the most harrowing ordeals in the history of navigation on Lake Superior.

The *Monarch* was a propeller-driven wooden steamship, 240 feet long and 35 feet in the beam, built in Sarnia, Ontario, in 1890. In 1906 she was engaged in transporting freight and passengers on Lake Superior. The *Monarch's* captain, thiry-eight-year-old Edward Robertson of Sarnia, was considered one of the best skippers on the Great Lakes. He had never had an accident. The *Monarch's*

Isle Royale, the largest island in Lake Superior, belongs to the United States, even though it is closer to the Canadian shore. Americans have Benjamin Franklin to thank for that. After the Revolutionary War, the border was being drawn between British North America and the newly independent United States. Franklin correctly believed that Isle Royale might hold rich mineral deposits. As the chief U.S. diplomat, he convinced the British that it was a useless rock, of no value to them. Thus, Isle Royale is now part of the state of Michigan, instead of the province of Ontario.

record was just as good; not a single accident in sixteen years of service. But all that was about to change.

On December 6, 1906, the *Monarch* left Port Arthur, bound for Sault Ste. Marie on her last scheduled trip of the season. She carried a cargo of wheat, oats, and flour. On board were ten passengers and a crew of thirty; all men except for the stewardess, a Mrs. Gregory. By the time the *Monarch* reached the Passage Island Strait, darkness had fallen and a snowstorm had blown in. Captain Robertson navigated his ship safely past the islands and deadly Canoe Rock. But when he headed out onto the open lake, he found conditions so bad that he decided to turn back and seek shelter in the lee of Isle Royale.

The captain was using the flashing beacon of the Passage Island lighthouse as a guide. Suddenly it was gone; lost in the swirling snow. Then the situation got even worse. The large concentrations of iron in the ground in much of the north Superior country and in islands like Isle Royale could sometimes play havoc with ships' compasses, rendering them useless. That happened to the compass in the *Monarch's* pilothouse just when the captain had greatest need of it. With no compass and with the lighthouse beacon gone, Captain Robertson was groping in snow-shrouded darkness.

He proceeded cautiously, but at about 11 p.m. the *Monarch* came to a sudden stop with a terrific jolt that shivered the vessel from bow to stern and knocked passengers and crewmen off their feet. The *Monarch* had struck a rock at the eastern tip of Isle Royale at a place called Blake Point, about five miles across the water from the Passage Island lighthouse.

The *Monarch's* hull was ripped open and water was rushing in. Almost from the moment of impact, the steamer began to list. Captain Robertson knew the ship was doomed. He had to get the people off as quickly as possible, but he faced a major problem.

About thirty feet of wild, foaming water lay between the *Monarch* and the shore. The ship's lifeboats already must have been beyond the reach of the crew, because only the *Monarch's* yawl was available to ferry the people, a few at a time, to the island. Captain Robertson did not think the *Monarch* would stay afloat long enough for him to get everybody off that way. For anyone to attempt to swim ashore would have been suicide. The situation called for fast thinking and desperate measures.

A crew member named Charles McLaughlin volunteered to have a rope tied around his waist so he could be swung from the sinking ship to a projecting rock on the island. If McLaughlin could get over there, he might be able to secure a rope that others could use to escape from the *Monarch*. Captain Robertson agreed to the plan.

The first attempt to swing McLaughlin to the rock didn't work. He swung back and slammed against the side of the ship. On the second attempt the rope broke and McLaughlin fell. Everyone thought the courageous sailor was done for. But somehow McLaughlin managed to grab hold of the rock. He pulled himself up, and shouted to his shipmates to throw him another rope. They did so, and he secured it to a tree.

Now the passengers and crew of the *Monarch* had two ways of getting to shore, neither of them very inviting. Going by lifeboat meant crossing hellish waters that could capsize the boat in an instant, leaving the occupants with little chance of survival. The other option was to use McLaughlin's rope. Those who did had to step off the *Monarch* and make a hand–over–hand crossing, suspended in the dark, with driving snow hitting their faces and numb hands clutching the rope while the wind tugged at their bodies. One slip meant certain death in the icy water below. Incredibly, all but one of the *Monarch*'s people made it across safely.

In times of emergency, according to both tradition and to maritime law, sailors are supposed to look after their passengers' safety first. This was upheld by the *Monarch*'s crew. But once the passengers were all ashore, a deck hand named James Jacques panicked. Afraid that he might be left behind, Jacques tried to jump into the yawl. He plunged into the dark water and did not come back up. His body was never recovered.

The *Monarch* did not sink as fast as Captain Robertson had feared it would. He stayed aboard until morning so he could make an inspection in daylight to ensure no one had been left behind. Then he went ashore in the yawl. Soon only the *Monarch's* pilothouse was visible above the water.

Now thirty-eight men and one woman were stranded on Isle Royale with nothing but the clothes on their backs. It was December, and the prospect loomed of death from exposure or starvation if they were not rescued. It was so late in the season, there might be no more ships passing through the strait. Even if one did, there was no guarantee the crew would see the people huddled on Blake Point. The survivors might as well have been on an Arctic island.

All that day and into the night a frigid, snow-laden wind blew. The men built a rough windbreak, but it provided little protection from the gale. The morning after that first terrible night one of the men found some dry matches in his pocket. The castaways started a fire to keep warm by, but found it difficult to keep it going in the wind and blowing snow. They hoped that the lighthouse keeper on Passage Island would see the fire and investigate. But Captain Robertson thought the snowstorm would probably hide the light. If only the weather would clear!

The storm howled for another day and night. As the miserable hours dragged by, some of the people began to suffer from frostbite, first in fingers and toes, and then in hands and feet. Everyone was weak from hunger. One man became seriously ill, probably from pneumonia. The castaways barely managed to keep their fire burning. The knifing wind swept its warmth away before it could restore feeling to numb hands. Finding and dragging firewood drained what little strength the fire-tenders had left. A few people suffered burns when they stumbled and fell right onto the fire.

On the morning of Sunday, December 9, the murderous wind finally eased up a little. Two or three of the crewmen risked going back to the wrecked *Monarch* to search for food. This was an extremely dangerous undertaking. The ship was impaled on a rock, with only the pilothouse above the water. The vessel was taking a pounding from heavy seas and could have slipped off the rock and sunk to the bottom at any moment. Nonetheless, the sailors somehow managed to find a bag of flour. The castaways used this to make hardtack biscuits, the first food they'd had in three days. This gave them at least a little strength. They would soon need it.

Over in the Passage Island lighthouse, two keepers were on duty, Alexander Shaw and Klass Hamringa. They saw smoke rising above Isle Royale. One of them – accounts do not say who – rowed across the strait in a small boat to investigate. He saw the people on the island, but could not approach the shore because the water was still too rough. Something must have happened to the castaways' yawl, because one of the men was compelled to perform a heroic act. Reginald Beaumont, the *Monarch's* purser, dove into the frigid water and swam out to the light keeper's boat. The water was cold enough to kill, but somehow Beaumont made it. He told the light keeper what had happened, and then both men hauled on the oars to get back to Passage Island.

The light keepers had no communication with the mainland. However, from the lighthouse they saw the steamer *Edmonton* come into sight. One of them rowed out to the ship and told the captain about the people stranded on Isle Royale. The *Edmonton* was too big to get in close to Blake Point, and the water still too rough for the skipper to send in the ship's boats. The captain did the only thing he could under the circumstances, and carried the news of the shipwreck to Port Arthur.

Two tugboats, the *Whalen* and the *Grace*, were dispatched to Isle Royale. The cold, hungry, desperate people cheered when they saw the tugs. But their ordeal was not over yet. They were on the south shore of Isle Royale's eastern tip. Because of reefs and heavy seas, the tugs could not approach their position. The nearest place where the tugs could get close enough to rescue the people was a little bay called Linis Harbor on the north shore. The tugs signaled that information to Captain Robertson.

Under winter conditions, with deep snow all the way, to walk from Blake Point to Linis Harbor would have been a challenge for fit and well-equipped hikers. For the haggard, frostbitten, exhausted survivors of the *Monarch,* it was a brutal three-hour trek through hell. The man who was too ill to walk had to be carried all the way, by people who could barely hold themselves up.

A few were on the brink of losing their minds. They wanted only to give up, lie down in the snow and go to sleep. Better to quietly die than endure another minute of icy torture!

Captain Edward Robertson kept them going. He had already lost one man, and he was determined not to lose one more soul. The captain had a frozen foot and a frozen hand, but he was the force that kept the people moving. He pulled people to their feet when they fell, and pushed them forward. He shouted until he was hoarse, urging the people to keep putting one foot in front of the other. He even threatened stragglers with violence if they didn't keep up. He would allow no one to stop or rest. To surrender to exhaustion was death! No doubt some of the stumbling wretched people cursed Captain Robertson, but he was saving their lives. He got every one of them to Linis Harbor, where the *Whelan* and the *Grace* were waiting.

The people were barely conscious as they were taken aboard the tugs. Mrs. Gregory fainted as soon as she stepped on board. Some of the men paced back and forth, sobbing unashamedly. The survivors were given food and warm blankets. Doctors were on board to treat frostbite and burns. Whatever their injuries, the refugees from the *Monarch* were thankful just to be alive.

Captain Robertson was completely cleared of any blame for the wreck of the *Monarch*. In fact, he was highly praised for his leadership and his determined efforts to get all of the crew and passengers off Isle Royale alive. A banquet was held for him in Port Arthur, and there was a big reception for him and some of the other survivors in his home port of Sarnia. The battered *Monarch* eventually broke up, slid off the rocks, and sank to the bottom of the strait. The wreck remains there to this day.

7

Strange Tale of the Success

Prison Ship

On the evening of July 4, 1946, the residents of Port Clinton, Ohio, on the south shore of Lake Erie, witnessed a blazing display that had nothing to do with that community's Fourth of July celebrations. Out on the lake, an ancient sailing ship that had run aground more than a year earlier was on fire. Many of the people watching the spectacle of a once-proud tall ship in flames perhaps considered it a fitting end to a derelict wreck. The United States Coast Guard had condemned the hulk as a hazard to navigation. Just who started the fire that ended the vessel's long history would never be known. It was a mysterious funeral fire for a ship that had once been a prison, and had become a legendary symbol of human cruelty.

The strange story of the *Success* began thousands of miles from Lake Erie, in Natmaw, Burma. According to legend, she was built there by the British for the East Indian trade in 1790. The *Success* was 135 feet long, 30 feet in the beam, and weighed over 600 tons. She was solidly constructed of Burmese teak, and was fitted out as a barkentine, a three-masted sailing ship with square sails on the foremast, and fore-and-aft sails on the other masts.

For the next twelve years, according to the legend, the *Success* plied the seas of the Orient, visiting ports-of-call that were the settings for tales of romantic adventure. She carried such exotic cargoes as ivory, spices, silks, jewels, rare woods, and Chinese tea. Occasionally she made the long voyage to London, England. It was during a visit to London in 1802, the story goes on to say, that the career of the *Success* was dramatically changed.

At that time, criminal law in England was extremely harsh. Hanging was the most common punishment – for offenses that would be considered trivial today. And even when many of these minor crimes were removed from the list of capital offenses, they were still punishable by long prison terms. Soon England's jails and prisons were overflowing. To relieve itself of the ever-growing prison population, the British government began shipping convicts to penal colonies in Australia. This practice also provided labor that could be used to exploit Australia's natural resources, as there were not many colonists who were willing to travel to a place as far away from England as Australia.

Several ships were converted into convict transports for the "felon fleet." The legend of the *Success* relates that she was one of those ships. For the prisoners locked in the hold of a convict ship for the long voyage to Australia, life was hell. The air below deck was foul with the odors of unwashed clothing and bodies, human waste, and bilge water. Many of the prisoners were seasick, and that added to the revolting smells. The food was vile, and after a few weeks at sea, the drinking water became scummy. Prisoners who were rebellious or who broke rules were subjected to whippings and other tortures. Many died at sea, and their bodies were dumped overboard without ceremony.

The legend of the *Success* is a grim one indeed, but it is not all true. Records show that the ship was built in Burma in 1840, not 1790. She was a merchant vessel trading in the Far East, and also made voyages to England and the West Indies. From 1847 to 1852 she transported immigrants from the British Isles to Australia. The voyage for those settlers was difficult, but it was not the living nightmare of the convict ships.

However, the *Success* did have a sudden change of duties. In 1851 a gold rush in Britain's Australian colony of Victoria brought a surge of immigrants. Like all gold rushes, the one in Australia also attracted a horde of criminals: thieves, confidence men, crooked gamblers, and bandits. Adding to the colony's troubles were the bushrangers — former convicts who had either escaped from captivity, or had been released at the end of their sentences and then fled into the Australian bush to live as outlaws.

The Victoria colony was soon experiencing the same problem that had plagued England. There was not enough room in the jails for all the convicted criminals. The solution was to use ships as "prison hulks." These ships were not transports. They lay at anchor far enough from shore to discourage escape, and were simply floating cell blocks in which prisoners were separated from the rest of the world by water instead of high walls.

In 1852, when the *Success* arrived at Victoria with a load of immigrants, most of her crew deserted to join the gold rush. With no men to sail their ship, the owners of the *Success* sold the vessel to the colonial government for use as a prison hulk. It was a sad fate for a proud ship, and the true beginning of the story that would end on Lake Erie.

Cells with iron bars were built into the *Success*. The gloomy hold that had once been occupied by immigrants full of hope for a new life was now a rat-infested dungeon for convicts whose lives were empty of hope. Conditions were horrible. The guards were often as brutal as the worst of the prisoners. Beatings were part of daily life. Medical facilities were non-existent, and many prisoners died. Guards were murdered when desperate prisoners tried to escape.

Some of Australia's most notorious bushrangers were incarcerated on the *Success*. One was Harry Power, an outlaw who had once been associated with Ned Kelly. Power had actually been a criminal mentor to Kelly, who went on to become the most infamous bandit leader in Australian history. Ned Kelly was eventually hanged for murder. Harry Power survived his long imprisonment for highway robbery and was released at the age of sixty-six.

By 1885, Australia had outgrown its role as a dumping ground for convicts, and law-abiding Australians considered the prison hulks to be unsightly reminders of a grim past. The government ordered them all to be broken up. But through a clerical error, the *Success* escaped destruction.

According to the story, many Australians resented the fact that the old prison ship was still afloat. Not only was the *Success* an unwanted relic of a brutal period Australians wanted to forget, but some people also claimed she was haunted. It was said that the cries and moans of tortured, despairing convicts could be heard coming from the empty ship at night. One day,

Ned Kelly (1835 – 1880) has been celebrated in legend, song, and film as an Australian Robin Hood. Many Australians consider him an outlaw hero, but most historians say he was a thief and a killer. His criminal career ended when home-made armor failed to protect him from police bullets, and capture.

the legend says, a group of men scuttled the *Success*. Thousands of people watching from shore cheered as she sank in 70 feet of water, where she remained for five years. However, there is no evidence that this actually occurred. Just what became of the *Success* for the next five years is a mystery.

The real tale picks up again in 1890, when a syndicate of entrepreneurs bought the *Success*. (They would have had to have her raised, if she had indeed been scuttled.) These men had the old ship towed to Sydney Harbour, had her painted and fitted with rigging, and turned her into a tourist attraction. They believed people would pay to visit a genuine prison ship and hear all about the horrors that had made the *Success* an object of fear. Wax figures of convicts were put in the cells. There were displays of various instruments of torture, as well as artifacts associated with the infamous Kelly gang. As a final touch of authenticity, the ship's owners hired Harry Power as a tour guide.

The white-haired former convict could chill the blood of visitors with his first-hand gruesome stories about life on a prison ship, and he would not have had to invent any tales. When he took his guests below deck to see the cells, he always hurried past cell number 24. That was the cage in which he himself had been confined for years. Apparently, Power's memories of that cell were so painful he could not stand to be near it for more than a few seconds.

Harry Power died within a year of becoming a tour guide on the *Success*. On the subject of Power's end, legend and fact once again clash. The legend says that Power was so tormented by dreams and memories of his convict days that he jumped overboard and drowned. However, the record shows that he drowned, probably after drinking too much, in the Murray River near the town of Swan Hill in 1891. No doubt the story of Harry Power gave rise to the tales about cell number 24 being the most haunted part of the *Success*.

After a successful tour of Australian ports, in 1895 the *Success* sailed to London to begin a series of tours of the British Isles. The ship was a popular attraction for several years, but by 1912 interest was diminishing. That year a Canadian captain named John Scott sailed the *Success* from Cork,

Ireland, to Boston, making her one of the oldest vessels known to have made the Atlantic crossing.

For three years the *Success* was a major draw in eastern American ports. Then in 1916 she sailed through the Panama Canal to become part of the Panama-Pacific Exposition in San Francisco. Upon her return to the Gulf Coast, the *Success* toured the Mississippi River System as far north as Pittsburgh. Finally, in 1923, the prison ship began her first tour of the Great Lakes.

The *Success* was a big hit at all the ports of call on the Inland Seas, particularly Chicago and Cleveland. Thousands of people climbed aboard to look at the displays of torture devices, peer into the cramped cells, and listen to the story of unfortunate Harry Power. The tour was made all the more creepy with the tales of ghosts, especially the one in cell 24. The men who worked on the ship claimed that at night they would not go below deck because they heard strange noises – and even saw ghostly arms protruding from the cell doors, as though prisoners were still in there, trying to get out.

After the *Success* had enjoyed several profitable years on the lakes, it became obvious to her owners that the old ship's time was running out. She had to be towed from port to port because seamen who knew how to work a sailing ship were becoming hard to find. The numbers of tourists dwindled. With less money coming in for maintenance, the ship began to deteriorate.

Most shipwrecks are sudden and dramatic, but the demise of the *Success* was a long, drawn-out ordeal. In 1943, while moored to a dock in the harbor of Sandusky, Ohio, the leaky old ship took on too much water during a storm and settled on the bottom, just a few feet below the keel. She sat there for about a year before a new owner named Walter Kolbe had the hull pumped out.

Kolbe had the *Success* towed to Port Clinton, where he intended to re-fit her as a tourist attraction and provide her with a permanent berth. But on the approach to the town's harbor, the *Success* ran onto a sandbar and was stuck fast, about half a mile from shore. Kolbe decided to leave the ship there for a season or two, while he looked into the possibility of having a channel dug through to the inner harbor. That decision was fatal to the *Success*.

The relentless pounding of Lake Erie's waves began to break the ship up. In the winter, grinding ice inflicted even more damage. Vandals sneaked out in the night to rob the ship of relics. Even her steering wheel and figurehead were looted. When Kolbe realized the situation of the *Success* was hopeless, he had no choice but to save what he could of his investment. He stripped the hulk of the valuable Burmese teak beams. He also took the blocks of Indian marble that were the original ballast, and the iron doors from the cells, which he sold as curiosity pieces. Now just an empty shell of the wreck lay awash on the sandbar.

The blaze of July 4, 1946, burned the *Success* down to the waterline. The submerged timbers were soon buried in sand. The ghost of cell 24, and all the other phantoms of the prison ship – if they had indeed haunted the vessel – were freed at last.

8

Wreck of the Edmund Fitzgerald

The Witch of November

When the freighter *Edmund Fitzgerald* was launched at River Rouge, Michigan, in 1958, she was the largest ship on the Great Lakes. "Big *Fitz*," as the vessel was nicknamed, was 729 feet long, 75 feet in the beam, and weighed 13,632 tons empty. She soon set several records for big freighters. Only the best and most experienced officers were hired for the *Edmund Fitzgerald*. Any Great Lakes sailor would have been proud to sign aboard.

For seventeen years the *Fitz* sailed the inland seas without incident. Nobody would ever have dreamed that the mighty *Edmund Fitzgerald* could be swallowed up by the deep, dark waters of Lake Superior.

On November 9, 1975, the *Fitz* prepared to leave the Burlington Northern Dock at Superior, Wisconsin. In the hold was a cargo of 26,116 tons of iron ore destined for the steel plant on Zug Island in the Detroit River. In the pilot-house was Captain Ernest McSorley, sixty-three, a top-rated skipper who had been with the ship since 1971. He had been a captain since 1951, and had said that the *Fitzgerald* would be his last ship. That statement would turn out to be tragically prophetic. First Mate John H. McCarthy, sixty-two, had supervised the loading of the ore. It was important that the weight of the bulk cargo be evenly distributed in the hold, or the ship would not ride properly in the water. A poorly balanced load could even cause the vessel to capsize.

Captain McSorley knew from long experience that November was a treacherous month for sailing the Great Lakes, especially Lake Superior. Sudden storms could quickly turn the lake into a monster as ferocious as the North Atlantic at its worst. There was not a sailor on the Lakes who did not dread the fearful "Witch of November."

Twenty-nine men were on the *Edmund Fitzgerald* when she steamed out of port that mid-afternoon. Captain McSorley was the oldest. The youngest was watchman Karl Peckol, age twenty. Most of the men were from Great Lakes states: Wisconsin, Michigan, Minnesota, Pennsylvania, and Ohio. Two crewmen were from Florida, and one was from California. The steward, Robert Rafferty, was aboard only because he was filling in for another man who was sick.

The day had dawned warm and sunny. The men might have hoped that the notorious autumn storms would hold off until they had crossed the lake and reached the locks at Sault Ste. Marie. However, Captain McSorley had received worrisome radio reports about the weather that lay ahead. The eastern part of Lake Superior was being lashed by gale force winds. McSorley was no stranger to November storms, and he had every confidence in his ship. But he did not realize that he was heading into the worst storm of the year.

Two-and-a-half hours after leaving port, the *Fitz* overtook the freighter *Arthur M. Anderson,* bound for Gary, Indiana. The *Anderson's* captain, Jesse Cooper, communicated with McSorley by radio. The two captains agreed that instead of taking the usual shipping lane through American waters, they would detour to the "north shore" route. That meant sailing close to the Canadian mainland, where they might find some shelter from the brunt of the storm. The *Fitzgerald* was the faster of the two ships, and soon left the *Anderson* behind.

By midnight the vessels were ten to fifteen miles apart. At 1 a.m., November 10, United States Coast Guard stations received a report from Captain McSorley. He was about twenty miles south of Isle Royale, encountering 10-foot waves, and rain and snow driven by 52-knot winds. Based on McSorley's information, the United States Weather Bureau radioed a heavy storm warning to all ships on the lake. Both the *Fitzgerald* and the *Anderson* received the warning, and continued on course at full speed. The *Anderson* was not as close to the Canadian shore as the *Fitzgerald.* Over the next few hours Captain Cooper closed the distance between them to seven to ten miles.

The two captains wanted to reach the relative safety of Whitefish Bay at the eastern end of Lake Superior. But with their ships being battered by howling winds, they opted for different approaches to Canadian waters. Captain Cooper was concerned about the shoals of Caribou Island, one of the most deadly ship-traps along the Canadian shore. He very cautiously picked his way through the dangerous waters between Michipicoten Island and Caribou Island, giving Caribou a wide berth. This caused him to fall about seventeen miles behind the *Fitzgerald*. Even though, "it was blowing a real gagger," as Cooper later described it, he managed to take the *Anderson* through safely.

In the hours it took him to execute his maneuver, Captain Cooper was in constant radio contact with Captain McSorley. He also had the *Fitzgerald* on his radar screen. The storm grew ever more violent. In fact, it was almost at hurricane status, and was wreaking havoc throughout the Great Lakes region, turning the freshwater seas into boiling cauldrons. The *Anderson* and the *Fitzgerald* experienced a brief calm as the eye of the storm passed over them. Then the assault of wind and water was renewed with even greater ferocity. Captain Cooper later reported that the *Anderson* was "taking a lacing, heading right into it and taking water on both sides."

To add to the captains' troubles, the radio beacons at Caribou Island and Whitefish Point were out of order, making it difficult for them to find direction. With visibility poor, they were practically sailing blind. Captain McSorley radioed other vessels, asking if anyone had picked up the White-fish Point Signal. This was the first indication that the *Edmund Fitzgerald* was in trouble.

As the day wore on visibility improved. But towering seas were crashing over the ships' decks. Angry dark clouds hung low over the lake. Captain Cooper fought to keep on a course that would ensure he would safely by-pass Six Fathom Shoal, one of the deadliest submerged rock formations off Caribou Island. The *Anderson* was fifteen miles behind the *Fitzgerald*.

At 3:20 p.m. Captain Cooper and his first mate, Morgan Clark, caught sight of the *Fitzgerald*. To their astonishment, the *Fitz* was too close to Six Fathom Shoal. Cooper told Clark that he wouldn't want the *Anderson* to be where the *Fitzgerald* was.

Fifteen minutes later, Captain McSorley called Captain Cooper. He said his ship had been damaged. The *Fitzgerald* had lost some fence railing and two ballast tanks, and was starting to list. Cooper asked, "Have you got your pumps going?"

McSorley replied, "Yeah, both of them. Will you shadow me down the lake? I'll reduce my speed so that you can overtake me."

"Okay," said Cooper. "We will do our best."

By now heavy snow was blowing again, and the men on the *Anderson* lost sight of the *Fitzgerald*. But they still had her on radar. The blip on the screen showed that the gap between the ships was slowly being closed.

Throughout the late afternoon and into the early evening McSorley kept up radio contact. He said his radar was out and he needed the *Anderson* to give him bearings. At 7:10 p.m., Captain Cooper was out of the pilothouse for a few minutes, so First Mate Clark took McSorley's call. In a calm voice Captain McSorley said, "I am holding my own. We're going along like an old shoe. No problems at all." These were the last words anyone heard from the *Edmund Fitzgerald*. Then the big ship simply disappeared from radar.

At this point the *Anderson* was nine miles behind the *Fitzgerald*. Captain Cooper thought at first that the weather was interfering with his radar. But his screen still showed several other ships that had been battling the storm. Within half an hour the storm died away, and suddenly Captain Cooper could see for miles around. He saw the running lights of ships as far as seventeen miles away. But where the *Edmund Fitzgerald* should have been there was nothing but darkness.

Captain Cooper turned to First Mate Clark and asked, "Where's the *Fitzgerald?*" Both men anxiously scanned the lake with binoculars. They thought the *Fitz* might have had a blackout, but that they might still see her silhouette against the night sky. There was nothing out there but water.

Captain Cooper checked the radar again. When that proved fruitless he began calling other ships in the area, asking if they could see the *Fitzgerald* or if they had her on radar. "There just wasn't anything," Cooper said later. "She was just gone."

The *Edmund Fitzgerald* sank in Canadian waters, and went down so quickly, no one on board had a chance to even send out a distress signal. Sailors the length and breadth of the Great Lakes were stunned by the news. Ships and aircraft from Canada and the United States conducted a massive search, and parties of men on foot patrolled the Ontario shoreline. They found some wreckage: two lifeboats, two rafts, several lifejackets, a few oars, and a floodlight from the *Fitzgerald's* pilothouse. They found no survivors; not even a single body. Quite likely Captain McSorley and all of his crew were entombed in the big steel freighter on the bottom of Lake Superior.

Underwater exploration eventually revealed that the *Edmund Fitzgerald* lay broken in half at a depth of more than 500 feet. Exactly what caused the sinking would be debated for many years. No one could say positively whether the ship broke up first and then sank, or sank first and then snapped in two when she hit the bottom. Based on Captain McSorley's last radio reports, the *Fitz* was already taking on water when he was talking to the *Anderson*.

There were several theories as to what caused the disaster. Any of them could have been possible. None could be absolutely proven. The *Fitzgerald* could have bottomed out and struck the rocks of Six Fathom Shoal, ripping a hole in her hull. She might have been swamped by huge waves. The hatches could have been improperly secured, allowing water to run into the hold. The ship could have been caught in a trough between two giant waves, causing her to break in two because of the weight of the ore in her hold. As the ship was being tossed by the storm, the tons of ore in the hold could have shifted, causing the ship to list and take in water.

For many years the story of the *Edmund Fitzgerald* was an unsolved mystery and the focal point of much controversy. Then in 2010, Great Lakes researchers finally concluded that Big *Fitz* had been swamped by a 50-foot rogue wave. Once thought to be only legend, rogue waves have been proven to be real, although rare. They occur when strong winds and powerful currents converge to create a wave twice as high as normal.

The loss of the *Edmund Fitzgerald* and the twenty-nine men aboard was one of the worst Great Lakes disasters of the twentieth century. It is a sad story that has become legendary, thanks in great degree to the song

In 1976 Canadian folksinger Gordon Lightfoot composed and recorded
the ballad "The Wreck of the *Edmund Fitzgerald.*" The song became one
of his biggest hits, and he performed it regularly in live concerts. However, some people objected to one line in the song that implied human
error was a factor in the disaster. After watching a documentary film that
showed how a rogue wave sank the ship, Lightfoot changed the contro-
versial line for subsequent live performances.

"The Wreck of the *Edmund Fitzgerald.*" Written and recorded by Canadian
folksinger Gordon Lightfoot, the ballad is a tribute to the men who died
when their ship became a victim of the Witch of November.

9

Creatures of the Abyss

Lake Ontario

Could there be monsters in the Great Lakes? Loch Ness in Scotland is famous for Nessie, the legendary Loch Ness Monster. Lake Champlain, which is mostly in the United States but has its northern end in Canada, is allegedly the home of a monster called Champie. Lakes Memphremagog and Massawippi in Quebec, and Lake Ogopogo in British Columbia are also said to have mysterious resident monsters. But these lakes are small compared to the vast bodies of water that make up the Freshwater Seas of central North America. If elusive monsters can lurk in their waters, how much more likely that strange creatures might be hidden in the depths of the Great Lakes!

Beneath the waves of Lake Ontario is a huge, dark abyss that could conceivably be the haunt of aquatic beasts that rarely venture near the surface. In First Nations folklore there are tales of such creatures. Recorded sightings of unusual reptilian "serpents" date back to colonial times. Not all of these documented incidents can be easily explained away.

The earliest known sighting of something strange in Lake Ontario waters came in July of 1817. The crew of an unidentified ship reported seeing a black, snake-like monster about three miles off the Canadian shore. They said it was "one foot in diameter and thirty to forty feet in length." The men were certain it was not a floating log.

Four years later, in the spring of 1821, some boatmen on the St. Lawrence River claimed to have seen what they called a sea serpent. They said it was swimming upstream toward Lake Ontario. Most people would have thought

With a surface area of 7,540 square miles, Lake Ontario is the smallest of the Great Lakes. But it occupies a very deep V-shaped chasm. Lake Ontario's maximum depth of 802 feet is greater than that of the more expansive Lake Huron. Lake Ontario's average depth of 283 feet is second only to that of Lake Superior and its volume of water is four times that of Lake Erie, which is broader but shallower.

the boatmen had overactive imaginations. But the following September the *Palladium*, a newspaper in Oswego, New York, reported that two men, John Maupin of Montreal and James Sigler of Jefferson County, New York, had seen the same creature. The men swore to a Canadian Justice of the Peace that their story was true.

On the morning of July 25, Maupin, Sigler and eight voyageurs were on Lake Ontario in the freight canoe *Lightfoot,* en route from Montreal to Mackinac. They were at a location one hundred miles east of Niagara, and twenty miles from shore. They saw what first appeared to be a burnt log floating about 500 yards ahead of them. They estimated the thing was 25 feet long.

As they drew closer, the men saw that the "burnt log" was actually an animal. It lay motionless, and seemed to be asleep. Then, when the canoe was less than 30 yards from the creature, the men got the fright of their lives. "The animal raised its head about 10 feet out of the water, looking around him in the most awful and ferocious manner, and darting forward with great velocity, making the water fly in every direction, and throwing columns of it at a vertical height of seven or eight feet with his tail. After having gone in a westward direction about one or two miles, he appeared to resume his former state, we then resolved to attack him, and accordingly loaded our guns for this purpose, and moved slowly toward him within gun shot."

The men now had a better view of the animal, and estimated it to be 37 feet long, and more than 2 feet in the thickest part of the body. It was covered with black scales, and had a tremendous snake-like head. A "large red and venomous looking tongue" flickered from the monster's mouth.

The would-be dragon slayers did not get a chance to shoot at the creature. This time as they approached it, the beast slid beneath the waves and out of sight. "After the animal disappeared," the witnesses said, "we continued our course with a lively oar, as may well be imagined."

Whatever it was that Maupin, Sigler, and the other men had seen, the creature remained hidden for another twelve years. The next lake monster story did not appear until July 1, 1833, when the Oswego *Palladium* carried "a tale of wonder." The story came from Captain Abijah Kellogg of the schooner *Polythermus*. The captain admitted that his account was incredible, but he insisted it was true.

On the evening of June 15, Kellogg's schooner was passing about two miles northwest of the Ducks (Main Duck and False Duck islands, in the eastern end of the lake). Suddenly the captain saw something that looked like a ship's mast floating off his bow. He was both surprised and alarmed to realize that it was not just drifting, but was moving on its own. Moreover, it was heading straight for his ship!

"Singing out to his hands to take care of themselves," the newspaper reported, "he put the schooner up to the wind, lashed the helm a lee, and run up the main rigging, waiting for the monster to approach. The serpent, for it was no other than an immense snake, neared the vessel and passed immediately under her stern, taking no notice whatever of the schooner or of those on board, but affording everybody an ample opportunity to observe and note his monstrous dimensions. In length he was about 175 feet, of a dark blue color, spotted with brown; towards either end he tapered off but about the middle his body was of the circumference of a flour barrel, his head was peculiarly small and could not be distinguished but from the direction in which he moved."

The creature, which swam with an undulating movement, was in sight of captain, crew, and three passengers for a full fifteen minutes before it vanished into the depths. It was heading in the direction of the St. Lawrence River. If Captain Kellogg's account was in fact true, and the newspaper quoted him accurately, the creature was the longest "serpent" ever seen on the Great Lakes.

Nine years passed before the strange creature was heard of again. The next report came in 1842 from Prince Edward County, the large, irregularly shaped peninsula that juts into the eastern end of Lake Ontario from the Canadian shore. Two brothers named McConnell were playing on the lakeshore near Gull Pond, not far from the village of Athol. They looked through a thicket of trees toward the lake and saw "a huge monster," which they described about the thickness of a man's body," a head proportionately large and very glossy; the eyes were about the size of a horse's and very bright."

The terrified boys ran home and told their father what they had seen. Mr. McConnell did not own a gun, so he sent for a friend, John Church, who had a rifle. The two men and the boys went looking for the monster. It was still where the brothers had seen it, just a short distance offshore. According to their account, the monster was, "blinking in the sun, his head about four feet out of the water. They judged him to be from 30 – 40 feet long, dark brown in color and a broad ring about his neck, varying in hue from the rest of the body."

While trying to get into a good shooting position, John Church apparently alarmed the beast, and it took to deeper water. The men and boys followed it for about two miles until they reached the Point Petre Lighthouse at the southwestern extremity of the peninsula. There they lost sight of the creature. The Prince Edward *Gazette,* which reported the incident, said, "We further learn that such a serpent has frequently been seen by people living along the lakeshore."

The town of Trenton is located on the Bay of Quinte, which separates Prince Edward County from the mainland. In September of 1864, the usually quiet community was disturbed by something more than just the sighting of a lake monster. Up until then, the serpents of Lake Ontario had been silent, but for the sounds of their bodies splashing in the water. This time the creature was vocal. The Belleville *Intelligencer* reported that a number of the inhabitants of Trenton had seen a sea-monster in the bay, but few people believed the stories. However, when a "perfectly reliable" man named Julius Baker claimed to have seen and heard the monster, the newspaper announced that the matter was "settled beyond any question."

"Not many days ago, while he and his wife were in a boat near the Indian Island, they were suddenly startled by a great splashing in the water and looking around discovered within about ten rods of the boat, the head and neck of a great serpent, about two feet out of the water. Mr. Baker describes the head to be in appearance like a bulldog, and says the snake was about 'three feet through.' Both were very much frightened, and immediately pulled for shore. Before reaching land the snake was seen three times, once only six yards from the boat, and again after they had landed only a few feet off. Mr. Baker said it followed him to shore, and made at times a dreadful noise. We may remark that the story is believed by some of the most respectful inhabitants to be true, they having the utmost confidence in the statements of Mr. and Mrs. Baker."

Some seventeen years later, on September 14, 1881, the steamer *Gipsy* was en route from Ottawa to Kingston when Captain Fleming and several crewmen and passengers saw a strange creature entering the Rideau Canal. Their story was reported in the Kingston *Whig*.

"The sportive creature made its appearance, of course, unexpectedly, and amazed the people with its immense proportions, unsightliness and graceless pranks in the water. The information respecting it is rather vague and indefinite, as is usual in such cases, but it is said to have appeared, according to the bias on which it was viewed, to be between 25 ft and 40 ft in length, to have a body of peculiar shape and great circumference, a head as big as a small house, numerous feet, and a tail so long and powerful that when in motion the water foamed and boiled up as a geyser and cast a spray which, one hundred yards distant, fell like heavy rain. The performance of this 'critter' was regarded in ominous silence. Once its fierce glittering eyes, canopied by sharp, flat horns, caught a glimpse of the steamer, and the serpent gave a tremendous lunge, the effect of which was to create a sea equal to that which the best gale on Lake Erie could not bring about."

Then, a year later, in August of 1882, the Toronto *Daily Mail* reported a "marine monster" in the lake off the Garrison Common. At that time Fort York was right on the lakeshore. Landfill has since left it a considerable distance inland. In his build-up to the monster story, the *Mail* journalist rather sarcastically stated that monsters seen in southern climates were larger than those seen in northern climates because the tropical heat of the low latitudes has such a magnifying effect on some brains that they see everything 'double.' The writer went on to say that owing to the coolness of the weather, the monster seen in Lake Ontario was not more than 50 feet long, and had the thickness of a man's body.

> "Between eight and nine o'clock, while placing the targets in position on No. 1 range, a boy rushed up saying that there was a queer thing floating near the shore. Some of the men were curious enough to leave their work and hasten down to the shore. There sure enough was a large, bluish-gray mass floating lazily near shore. It had every appearance of being asleep, as its body yielded to every ripple. Part was submerged, but the upper portion of the head floated just above the water."

The men claimed that they watched the creature for more than three minutes. They said that it was covered with short, stiff bristles, and that the part of the back that was visible above the water was lighter colored than the head. It had small eyes. The creature suddenly raised its head, swished its long tail, gave a short, sharp bark, and swam away.

The *Mail* writer concluded, "The men did not appear at all anxious to speak of the matter, as they feared their veracity would be questioned. As it is, their story is given for what it is worth, but surely the word of three men who saw it is worth that of thirty who did not see it."

There was another series of sightings off Kingston in June of 1888. The Kingston *Whig* reported, "The sight of it (the monster) has created alarm and the people in the locality are scared about going near the water . . . It is said that the serpent has been seen before. It is big enough to carry off a baby."

In all of these instances the monster had not demonstrated any sort of threatening behavior. That changed in July of 1892 when a Mr. G. Parks and his wife were sailing in a skiff near Kingston. The Toronto *Globe* reported their terrifying experience.

> "A serpent of huge proportions was heading for the boat. It held its head in the air and its eyes looked like balls of fire. It meant business, and Mr. Parks knew that if he did not make a defense he and his wife might be upset. Mr. Parks had a fish pole with him, and waited for the reptile. When it got near the boat the attack began, but Mr. Parks soon found out he had a mighty opponent. He had to pound the serpent for a long time before it would give up its attack. Finally it turned and disappeared in the water, making a noise like a buzz saw. Mrs. Parks was greatly frightened."

Repeated sightings of something strange in the water off Kingston led to the creature being nicknamed Kingstie. There were also further claims about unusual beasts cruising the Toronto region lakeshore. But nothing matched the near-hysteria of July and August of 1931, which became known as "The Summer of the Sea-Serpent."

On July 18, "Curly" Rhue and Bert Todd of Brantford were camping at Oshawa's Lakeview Beach, east of Toronto, when they saw a "commotion" out on the water. Rhue thought it was an exceptionally large fish or a school of carp, but Todd was certain that he saw a sea serpent, at least 30 feet long. Their story made the newspapers, and by the next evening reports of more monster sightings were reaching the press. Some people said they had shot at the beast, but their bullets didn't hurt it.

Skeptical newspaper editors suggested the monster might be British Columbia's Ogopogo, on a tour of the country. A Toronto *Globe* journalist asked, "What is this sea-serpent? Not an animal, not a fish, and not a snake. Each year sees some change in its make-up. For the Oshawa show it adopted a great hirsute head which was carried majestically across the water . . . The old explanation of the scoffers does not hold in regard to the sea-serpent, as it has been seen under various liquor regulations."

On July 22, some swimmers at the Oshawa beach brought ashore a 50-foot-long log covered with seaweed. That, they said, was probably what had caused all the excitement. People who claimed to have seen the beast did not agree. They argued that no log could have moved through the water as swiftly as the thing they had seen. Then two residents of Port Hope said they had seen the monster just off the shore of their community two days before the first Oshawa sighting.

On the evening of the 23rd, two boys were fishing off the pier at Whitby, to the west of Oshawa. They reported seeing, "a strange aquatic monster . . . swimming slowly along in the water about 50 yards from shore. The monster at times appeared to have three heads."

For a few days the monster made no appearances. Then on July 27 it reared its fearsome head in the waters off Main Duck Island. A fisherman claimed he saw a creature 40 feet long, and 18 inches thick. The next day the creature was seen by two Toronto residents while they were sailing off the Scarborough Bluffs. They said it glided along the surface close to their boat, and was visible for a whole minute. It was heading for Toronto.

Torontonians piled onto the Toronto Islands ferries in hope of seeing the creature as it cruised past the city. Crowds of people went to the Eastern and Western Gaps of Toronto Harbour in case the monster decided to swim right up to the waterfront. The beast did not oblige. However, children began making "sea-monsters" out of logs and towing them through the water with ropes.

Then on August 1, a sea-monster appeared just west of Toronto. The Port Credit beach was crowded that Saturday afternoon. Besides the many bathers and picnickers who had gone to the shore to escape the heat, a team of marathon swimmers was there, training for a competition. At dusk, two of those swimmers dashed out of the water and gasped that they had seen the sea serpent. The young men said the beast was at least 10 feet long, and had a great shaggy head.

The story quickly spread up and down the beach. Other people said they had seen the monster, too. They said it had green eyes, and a huge tail that swished back and forth as it swam. People who were in the water scrambled to get to the safety of dry land.

Ambrose Adams, the caretaker of the park, was skeptical. As darkness was falling over Lake Ontario, he set out in his rowboat to investigate. Just in case there *was* something out there, he took along a crowbar. The crowd, not sure if Adams was brave or crazy, waited breathlessly on shore. Someone called a newspaper to send a reporter.

A little while later, Adams rowed out of the darkness in his little boat. He coolly announced that the danger had passed. He said he had captured the monster and tied it to the Port Credit Lighthouse, which was a short distance offshore. Anticipating the scoop of the century, the reporter borrowed a flashlight and commandeered a boat. When he reached the lighthouse he saw the "serpent" that Ambrose Adams had captured. It was a child's wooden rocking horse with a long tail of seaweed attached to it.

The story of the hoax made the papers. Skeptics said the head of the toy horse was what people had seen bobbing around in the lake. Now, they sighed, there would be an end to the "sightings" of monsters. But others would not give up their belief in what they were sure they had seen with their own eyes. Just because some swimmers had been fooled by a rocking horse did not mean that there wasn't a monster in Lake Ontario. People continued to go to the lakeshore, hoping for a glimpse of the beast.

Summer's heat gave way to the cool days of autumn, and the serpent craze died down. Then, on October 12, there was a sighting by none other than the Port Credit Fire Chief, William Newman. He and his son-in-law, William Duncan, reported that they had, "without any mistake," seen the creature about 100 feet from shore.

"We were standing on the shore close to the Port Credit Lighthouse," Chief Newman said, "when we sighted the serpent coming toward us, and traveling at something like 30 miles an hour. It had a large, green head, resembling that of a lion, and would be about 20 feet in length." The Chief said that the creature swam a zigzag course, and caused the water to foam around it. Once again people flocked to the shore, hoping to see the monster. But the creature never made a return appearance. The Summer of the Serpent was over.

10

A Monster Called Bessie

Lake Erie

Over the years, sightings of a giant "serpent" in Lake Erie have given rise to the legend of a monster that has come to be known as Bessie. But could the relatively shallow waters of Lake Erie actually hide such a creature? It would seem so, because the reports date back almost two centuries.

The first known recorded sighting of a serpent in Lake Erie came in July of 1817. The crew of an unidentified schooner claimed to have seen a strange animal about five miles from shore. They said it was almost 40 feet long, and dark in color. A scientist who read the account said that the sailors had probably seen a gigantic eel.

But shortly after the July sighting, the "Water Snake of Lake Erie," as newspapers called the creature, was seen again. This time the observers said it was 60 feet long, copper-colored, with bright eyes. These people said they shot at the monster, but their musket balls had no effect. They were not sure if they missed, or if the creature was protected by scales.

More than half a century passed before the next documented account of a Lake Erie monster. In July of 1873, there was an extraordinary report of a sea serpent. It was followed by a dramatic close encounter out on the lake.

A gang of men working on a railroad near Buffalo, New York, claimed to have seen a monster, 20 feet long and 20 inches thick, in the lake. One of them said, "It must have been part whale, because occasionally it would spout water from its nostrils as high as 20 feet above its head . . . Its eyes were small and piercing and its mouth was broad with two rows of teeth." The witnesses added that the creature looked like a fish, had a tail, and traveled at about 10 miles an

Lake Erie has a surface area of 9,940 square miles, but it is the shallowest of the Great Lakes. It is 210 feet at its deepest point, and has an average depth of only 62 feet. But Erie is also a notoriously stormy lake, and because it is so shallow, its waters are usually murky with churned up sediment. Murky enough to conceal mysterious creatures?

hour. The strange beast disappeared as quickly as it had appeared. There would soon be evidence that the monster was amphibious.

Within a few days of the railroad gang's report, local farmers along the lakeshore began missing calves, sheep, and poultry. There was no evidence of wolves or human livestock thieves. The farmers were baffled. Then one farmer discovered strange tracks and marks on the ground that indicated an animal had been dragged down to the shore and into the water. The farmers came to the conclusion that the monster they had recently heard about had been preying on their livestock. There was only one thing to do; hunt the beast down and kill it!

The men chartered a tugboat, and a posse of men armed with rifles and shotguns went out monster hunting. They patrolled the area where the creature had been seen, certain that it must be lurking thereabouts. Watchful eyes scanned the surface in all directions. Trigger fingers twitched in nervous anticipation of a serpent suddenly leaping out of the water. Then someone shouted that he had seen something move in the water. The men cut loose with a barrage of bullets and buckshot. The waters churned and foamed. With a hideous scream the great serpentine head of the monster rose from the lake, its eyes "blazing like coals." For a few seconds it thrashed around in the foaming water, and then it sank from sight.

The triumphant men went ashore and announced that they had killed the monster. A local newspaper editor dismissed the whole episode as either a hoax or the result of too much whiskey. But the monster hunt did not end the sightings of strange creatures in Lake Erie. If the men had indeed killed a lake monster, a few years later there would be evidence of more of them.

On July 30, 1880, the crew of the schooner *General Scott* reported that they had seen a sea serpent about thirty miles from Erie, Pennsylvania. They described it as being nearly 40 feet long, with a neck that was 10 or 12 inches in diameter. The skin, they said, was like dull mahogany – nearly black. The creature swam very close to the schooner for a whole minute. The lake's surface was smooth, the men said, and they could see the thing clearly.

Nothing more was reported until May of 1877. At a French settlement on Locust Point in Ottawa County, Ohio, two brothers named Dusseau made a startling discovery as they returned from fishing. Approaching the shore, they saw a large phosphorescent mass lying on the beach. They secured their boat, and then went to investigate. Describing it later, the men said it was "a lake monster, writhing in agony." This "unknown fish of mammal size" resembled a large sturgeon, but "it had long arms which it threw wildly in the air." The fishermen said it was 20 to 30 feet long.

The brothers were frightened, but as they looked on, the creature apparently died. They hurried off to get a rope so they could drag the body further up the beach. Unfortunately, when they returned the monster was gone. The "dead" creature had somehow managed to roll back into the water. The only evidence left behind were some scales the size of silver dollars. Sturgeons don't have scales.

The monster was not heard of again until July of 1892 when the schooner *Madeline* arrived in Toledo, Ohio, with a fantastic tale. The skipper, Captain Woods, said that one hundred and thirty miles east of Toledo he and his crew saw the water ahead of them being lashed into foam. As they drew near, they were astonished to see "a huge sea-serpent wrestling about in the waters as if fighting with an unseen foe . . . It soon quieted down and lay at full length on the surface of the water."

According to Captain Woods, the serpent was, "about fifty feet in length and not less than four feet in circumference of body. Its head projected from the water about four feet." The captain said the creature was, "a terrible looking object. It had viciously sparkling eyes and a large head. Fins were plainly seen, seemingly sufficiently large to assist the snake in propelling itself through the water. The body was dark brown in colour, which was uniform all along."

People often doubted reports of sea monsters made by mariners. Sailors had a reputation for being superstitious, telling tall tales, and indulging in too much grog in the taverns. But in October of 1894, many people were inclined to believe the amazing account of a Protestant clergyman.

Reverend Alex Watt was pastor of the Baptist Church in Silver Creek, New York, a village on the Lake Erie shore, west of Buffalo. One day he, his wife, and another woman were strolling on the beach when they saw something that had them "paralyzed with astonishment." Not far from the shore was a creature with its head projected about 15 feet above the surface of the lake. They could not tell how much of it was hidden in the water. Running down the serpent's back were two rows of fins about a foot apart. The fins were a foot long. The creature had a large head and dark coloring. It was moving at about 10 miles an hour. As the amazed people watched, the monster dove into the water and vanished.

Several newspapers, including the Toronto *Globe,* carried the story of the sighting. The author of the *Globe* article concluded, "Considerable doubt has hitherto been thrown upon the statements of those who plainly witnessed this uncanny monster, but the truth of this latest report cannot be doubted." The reasoning here was that clergymen did not indulge in alcohol, falsehoods, or wild fantasies.

Not quite two years later, in May of 1896, the serpent appeared on the Canadian side of the lake. At Crystal Beach, near Fort Erie, Ontario, four people were sitting on a rocky point when they saw a "commotion" out on the water. The disturbance was too large and continuous, they thought, to be caused by one fish, so they thought it must be a school of fish in some kind of a frenzy. But as the "commotion" came nearer to the shore, one woman exclaimed, "Why, it is all one fish!" All agreed that it was indeed one large creature, moving across the water toward the beach.

One of the witnesses was a ship's captain named Beecher. He told a reporter for the St. Catharines *Daily Standard* that his party had more than "a mere fleeting glance of the serpent." They watched it for a full forty-five minutes until darkness fell and the creature swam out toward the open lake. "The surface of the lake was comparatively smooth," said Beecher. The beast was so near to his party, he claimed, that they could distinctly see its eyes, which looked as large as silver dollars.

"At times it would be straight on the surface of the water with its whole length visible. Then it would lift its head and curl its body so that it would be visible only at intervals, where the humps projected above the surface. At times it would turn partly on its side, when it was plainly seen that the colour of the lower part of its body was much brighter than the back, which was dark brown or almost black. Its head looked like a dog's head, having a similar prominence above and back of the eyes. Its tail, however, was pointed, and like that of any monstrous land serpent."

Captain Beecher threw stones in the creature's direction, and it would lunge as much as 30 feet to try to catch them, as though it thought they were food. The monster twisted and turned in different directions as it tried to catch the stones, sending up great spouts of water. If Beecher's story is true, it must be the only incident in Great Lakes history of a man playing with a sea serpent as though it were a dog. The captain said he didn't know if the monster was nervous or actually enjoying itself as it kept "sloshin' around" in the water. He swore that the creature was 35 feet long.

Sometime after the Crystal Beach sighting, a boy named C.D. Woolley was loading hay on his father's farm near Port Dover, Ontario. He was on a bluff above the lake. He looked across the water and saw "a hideous monster" about half a mile out. Nine feet of its body was out of the water, and it carried its head in a "reptilian manner." Woolley guessed that the beast was at least 30 feet long. He became very excited and called to his brother Will. But by the time Will arrived, the creature was gone. The brothers spoke to two neighbors who said they had seen the creature, too. However, for many years these people did not tell anyone about what they had seen, out of fear of being ridiculed.

Such was the case in the early twentieth century when the crew of a tugboat saw a monster off Long Point. The beast had "a head like a horse." The crew protested when the skipper of the tug began to chase the monster.

To their relief, the creature dove beneath the waves and did not reappear. The men did not tell anyone about this incident until about twenty years later.

Throughout the twentieth century there were numerous alleged monster sightings on Lake Erie. Most of them were dismissed as hoaxes, or skeptics said that the people in question had mistaken large sturgeons for sea serpents. But a music composer and former court reporter named Mary was certain that what she saw – and smelled – one July morning in 1983 was neither a hoax nor an oversized fish.

Mary's family had a cottage at the tourist resort of Rye Beach, just east of Sandusky, Ohio. She had been spending her summers there since she was a teenager. Mary knew that part of the lake well – or at least, she thought she did. She awoke early that summer morning, but couldn't get back to sleep, so she went outside to sit in a rocking chair by a breakwall. "It was about 5 a.m.," she recalled for *Toronto Star* reporter Michael Tenszen during an interview in January of 1991. "The lake was thick with fog and very placid. I heard a paddling sound, like some fishermen were out rowing early. Then I saw what looked like a capsized rowboat, very long, moving along. There was a huge back on this thing, like a turtle's back. It was about 30 to 35 feet long. It was real dark green. I smelled this stench, like rotten garbage.

"I froze. I never screamed – because I didn't have a voice. It got way out there, and then I saw a gigantic swan's or snake's head. It was awesome! It looked prehistoric."

Mary said that she could see one eye, and a mouth that appeared to be contorted into a grin. The beast seemed to be splashing playfully in the water. It made no threatening movements. Nonetheless, the woman was terrified.

"When it disappeared, the smell was gone. I ran into the house and bolted the door and prayed." Two years passed before Mary told anyone about her experience. "I really didn't think anybody would believe me," she explained.

More sightings followed. In the summer of 1985 some boaters saw a dark brown serpent with a flat tail off Vermilion, Ohio. They reported seeing five humps raised above the water. "No way that was a sturgeon," one of them insisted.

Days later a man saw what might have been the same creature near the Lorain Coast Guard Station, just east of Vermilion. The water was calm, the witness said, and he watched the "serpentine" animal for three or four minutes. He said it was twice as long as his 16-foot boat.

Over the next few years there continued to be reports of monster sightings on Lake Erie, especially along the western end of the American shore. Up until that time the creature had been nameless, although a few people referred to it as Lem, for Lake Erie monster. Then *The Beacon* of Port Clinton, Ohio, held a contest and bestowed the name South Bay Bessie on the creature. Most Lake Erie monster buffs would settle on "Bessie."

Throughout the 1990s and into the twenty-first century, people kept reporting sightings of Bessie. Those who swore they had seen the monster included Canadian and American fishermen, a Canadian agricultural worker, a pair of American fire inspectors, an American charter boat operator whose tale was supported by his wife and four passengers, and a veteran U.S. Navy man who was out in a boat with his wife and adult son. The man wanted to get closer to the creature for a better look, but his wife and son had no such desire. "Dad, let's go," his son said. "That thing looks bigger than us, Dad, and I'm not going to stay here to find out." The man later told a newspaper reporter, "I thought it was a whale at first, and I've seen some pretty big things in the ocean."

In August of 2001, a series of strange attacks shook the town of Port Dover, Ontario. Within a twenty-four hour period a man, a woman, and a child were viciously bitten on the legs while swimming at a location just outside of town. The attacks came without warning. "I just felt a great big chomp," said the woman.

A doctor who had extensive knowledge of Lake Erie's aquatic life was puzzled by the wounds. He said the bites were major – 6 inches between the punctures made by the upper and lower teeth. He ruled out snapping turtles, lamprey eels, walleye, goby fish, and muskellunge. People in the town began joking that Bessie was responsible for the bites, although the victims didn't think there was anything funny about it. The doctor thought a more likely explanation was that a bowfin had attacked the swimmers.

The bowfin, like the sturgeon, is a "living fossil." It is the sole survivor of a species that thrived millions of years ago. Sometimes called a dogfish, the bowfin is a voracious predator and is equipped with sharp teeth. The male can grow up to two feet in length. After spawning, the male bowfin aggressively defends the nest, attacking anything that comes near, including humans. "If it was indeed a bowfin that attacked the swimmers," said the doctor, "it was a big honking fish!" Or was it Bessie?

Bibliography

Barry, James, *Georgian Bay: the sixth great lake,* Clark, Irwin & Co, Toronto, 1968

Boyer, Dwight, *Great Stories of the Great Lakes,* Dodd, Mead & Co, New York, 1966

– *Ghost Ships of the Great Lakes,* Dodd, Mead & Co, New York, 1968

– *True Tales of the Great Lakes,* Dodd, Mead & Co, New York, 1971

– *Ships and Men of the Great Lakes,* Dodd, Mead & Co., New York, 1977

Butts, Edward, *Outlaws of the Lakes,* Lynx Images, Toronto, 2004

– *Guiding Lights, Tragic Shadows: Tales of Great Lakes Lighthouses,* Lynx Images, Toronto, 2005

Colombo, John Robert, *Mysterious Canada,* Doubleday Canada Ltd., Toronto, 1998

– The Monster Book of Canadian Monsters, Colombo & Co., Toronto, 2004

Firth, Edith G. (Ed.), *The Town of York, 1793 – 1815,* University of Toronto Press, 1962

Floren, Russell and Andrea Gutsche, *Ghosts of the Bay,* Lynx Images, Toronto, 1998

MacInnis, Dr. Joseph, *Fitzgerald's Storm: The Wreck of the Edmund Fitzgerald,* Macmillan Canada, Toronto, 1997

Malcomson, Robert, *Lords of the Lake: the Naval War on Lake Ontario, 1812 – 1814,* Robin Brass Studio, Montreal, 1998

Stonehouse, Frederick, *Went Missing,* Avery Color Studios, Gwinn, Michigan, 1993

Acknowledgments

The author would like to thank: Michael McAllister, Coordinator of the *Hamilton* and *Scourge* Project at the Hamilton, Ontario, Military Museum; the on-line Great Lakes Shipwreck File; the Ontario Provincial Archives; the Guelph Public Library, and the people at Tundra Books who continue to entrust me with projects like this one.

Photo Credits